Media commentator, speaker and writer Melinda Hutchings is passionate about helping teenagers overcome the issues and challenges they face. Author of *Why Can't I Look the Way I Want?*, Melinda is an inspiring role model and mentor who is intimately aware of how best to communicate with teenagers and their parents. She runs self-esteem programs for teens and frequently addresses schools, forums and conferences in Australia and overseas. For more information, visit Melinda's website www.melindahutchings.com.

It Will Get Better

It Will Get Better

Finding your way through teen issues

Melinda Hutchings

inspired
LIVING

ALLEN&UNWIN

First published in 2010

Inspired Living, an imprint of
Allen & Unwin
83 Alexander Street
Crows Nest NSW 2065
Australia
Phone: (61 2) 8425 0100
Fax: (61 2) 9906 2218
Email: info@allenandunwin.com
Web: www.allenandunwin.com

Cataloguing-in-Publication details are available
from the National Library of Australia
www.librariesaustralia.nla.gov.au

ISBN 978 1 74237 113 9

Internal design by Christabella Designs
Set in 11/16 pt Minion Pro by Bookhouse, Sydney

10 9 8 7 6 5 4 3 2 1

To Mum and Dad
with love and gratitude, always

Contents

Introduction

Sometimes life can twist and turn and take us places we hadn't expected. People let us down, friends disappoint us or we make stupid choices. Even with the best laid plans, things can change in a moment's notice or life doesn't always turn out the way we'd hoped.

But whatever you're facing, no matter how shocking or painful it may seem, there is always a solution. And the great thing is that you are not alone—other people have been there before you and understand what you are going through. There're also wonderful experts out there who know exactly what needs to be done to help you get back on track. Along with love and support from parents, wider family members, mentors, friends and those who have been through the same situation and come out on top, there's nothing too hard or embarrassing to face.

I know this, because I have faced some pretty tough issues and waded through the depths of loneliness and despair. Feeling lost and alone is one of the hardest places to be. But I found my way through, and you can too.

I'm here to say that it *will* get better—here's how.

Chapter 1

SOMETIMES BAD STUFF HAPPENS . . . BUT YOU'RE GOING TO BE OKAY

Many of the people who call Kids Helpline complain that no-one is listening to them.

You may also feel that you are not being listened to by the people in your life who count.

The aim of this book is to give you a 'crystal ball' so you know that although sometimes bad things happen, it doesn't mean you're a bad person, and there is always a way forward. Between these pages you will find stories from people just like you, who have suffered through terrible situations, felt lost and alone, been knocked sideways by something unexpected, done crazy things—and have managed to find their way through despite difficulty and hardship.

It is normal to feel stressed out, misunderstood, left out and confused sometimes. Over the weeks and months as I wrote this book, every time I turned around I discovered another heartbreaking story; someone left for dead by drug-addicted parents; others plucked from the familiarity of home and sent to an unknown place with strangers, or bullied and made to feel like crap for no good reason. But the common thread was the feeling that no-one cared enough to really listen.

It can be tough to make friends and find your place on the popularity scale; plan a future and wonder if it's the right path; resist drugs, alcohol and harmful behaviours. There is also the anxiety we all feel when we want to fit in and be accepted. In the background, our family and the way we are brought up play a role in who we become and the choices we make for ourselves and our future.

This book has been a process of evolution, during which I have been inspired by the courage and determination of the people I have interviewed. Their unrelenting will to keep going, to do their best even in the toughest of circumstances, to never give in no matter how painful life becomes, at times moved me to tears.

Many of the people I interviewed felt worthless. They didn't care about the future or were angry at the world. But more than that, they felt unloved.

You deserve to be loved and nurtured, to be given every chance of blossoming into someone with a strong sense of self-esteem and enthusiasm for life and the future.

It doesn't matter if you have one parent or two, a blended family, grandparents or other carers, as long as you have a sense of belonging and wellbeing you have every chance of thriving.

In a world where there is conflict, confusion and a lack of emotional security, it is my personal belief that we need to be true to what is in our hearts and believe in who we are.

As well as including personal stories that explore destructive behaviours and difficult circumstances, this book also profiles organisations filled with wonderful people who have chosen to work in this area because they care. They have the knowledge and experience to know what you need to get back on track, and are there because they are passionate about making life better for you.

On a personal note, although I suffered hardship as a teen, I have chosen to turn that into something positive by using that experience to empower and inspire others. So I wrote this book to show you how you can create a wonderful life, no matter what your circumstances.

My message is this: Always do your best, never make assumptions and live the life that is true to your heart. The key to happiness and inner peace is knowing who you are and never compromising that.

And when you feel alone and confused, or that no-one is listening, pick up this book and read these words again—and know that you are holding it in your hands because you are not alone.

From my heart to yours,

Melinda Hutchings

~ Love goes toward love ~

William Shakespeare

In profile: Alexis

Age: 19

Hair colour: Blonde

Eye colour: Blue

Favourite sayings: 'Yeah right' or 'Whatever'

Greatest personal moment: I love to make people have a great day. I hate seeing people down and I always make the effort to make them smile.

Dream yet to accomplish: Become a primary school teacher

Favourite colour: Pink

Favourite place in the world: Canada because my niece and nephew live there

Best tip: Stress less

Dream for my future: To be happy and always with the people I love

Best moment: When I realised how wonderful it felt *not* to be a victim. Once I figured that out I developed more confidence. People no longer walked all over me. I no longer felt afraid of what others would say if I stood up to them.

Chapter 2

DEALING WITH FAMILY BREAK-UPS

When parents fight and split

It's scary when your parents fight. And even more terrifying if they decide to break up. Suddenly everything changes and there's nothing you can do except go along with it all. Feeling scared is okay because everything will feel so unreal and for a time you may even wonder if your parents will get back together and everything will go back to normal. But what if they don't get back together? What are you supposed to do, and how do you decide whether to live with your mum or dad? Sometimes the decision is made for you by the courts, or your parents will have already decided.

Either way, your world is about to change and it's not going to be easy. As with any massive life-change there will be a period of adjustment where you will feel unsettled and overwhelmed. Your emotions will probably go up, down, sideways and in between as you cope with what happens after your parents split up. You may even get caught in the crossfire.

Through the tears and heartache, remember that you don't have to bear this by yourself. What you experience will be different to what someone else experiences because no two families are the same. Support from your closest friends and an impartial person such as the school counsellor can help as you vent your feelings. There is no right or wrong way to feel—how you feel is how you feel so don't be afraid if your emotions become intense and you feel completely devastated. Give yourself time to adjust and let your parents know how you are feeling. Ask questions so you understand what's going on and that it's not your fault. And remember that you will get through this and when you do, a sense of 'normal' will return.

Melinda

VIVID MEMORIES

My parents divorced when I was four. I still have vivid memories of them fighting all the time. My father was ill; his heart stopped three times. My mother couldn't handle it and so she left him while he was still in hospital.

Natashia

I MISS FAMILY NIGHTS

When I was younger, the thing I loved the most was Saturday nights at home, because it was family night. We'd all sit together and play Monopoly or watch videos. I really looked forward to Saturday nights. But then my parents started to argue and Dad left when I was five. I felt really sad and, growing up, Saturday nights were never the same again.

I was too young to understand what had happened and naturally, as children do, I started to form my own conclusions. It was such an emotionally intense experience, that I needed to make sense of it. I took on the blame and wondered, *What's going to happen to my world now?*

Tom

I WET THE BED UNTIL I WAS ELEVEN

I couldn't control it, no matter how I tried. From a young age Dad put me to bed and I'd fall asleep with my hand on his leg. The second I felt him move I'd wake up. When he was away on business I wet the bed and after he left Mum, it went on. I felt embarrassed about it, and upset because it meant I couldn't sleep over at a friend's house.

It finally stopped when I learned that I had to take care of myself.

Still to this day, I can't sleep next to someone without waking up when they move.

Alexis

RUNNING AWAY WAS MY ONLY ESCAPE

When I was young my parents moved us around a lot so I was always somewhere different, having to make new friends. We finally settled in one place, but then Mum and Dad started to fight. When the arguments grew worse I couldn't take it anymore and started running away from home.

My mum and dad eventually split up and my mother remarried not long after. But my stepfather verbally and physically abused me. He abused Mum too, which made me angry. Sometimes it got so bad that I'd have to call the police. Mum had an apprehended violence order put out on him, but ended up taking him back.

I didn't want to be at home so I kept away and stayed with friends. I lost contact with Mum for a while but at the time I didn't care. I used alcohol as a way to forget about it all.

Justin

WHEN DAD LEFT HOME

My parents split up when I was three, only a few months after my little brother was born.

A nasty custody battled followed and there was one incident when Dad tried to kidnap my brother, which was awful. I was frightened of my dad. He had a mean streak and often snapped for no reason.

After they split up, Mum forced me to see Dad because I had to see him a certain amount of days a year in order for her to receive maintenance payments.

I could tell that Dad hated me because he only ever ignored me, yelled at me or hit me. He wanted three sons and ended up with two sons and a daughter. He tried to make me like a boy by dressing me in similar clothing to my brothers, and then he'd chastise me and say, 'Why do you look like a boy when you're a girl?' A few times he became physically violent with me and this made me feel degraded, like I wasn't worth the attention and love my brothers received.

Dad remarried a year after he and Mum broke up. I didn't get along with my stepmother. She was physically violent with my older brother, and picked fights with me. My older brother became violent with me and my younger brother, and I had no choice but to learn how to defend myself. Sometimes we'd have horrific fights when we'd end up in a brawl, punching and hitting each other, and I'd retreat to my room, bruised and in tears.

When I turned fourteen I had the legal choice whether to see my dad or not, and I chose not to.

At home, Mum sits outside most of the time, drinking, smoking and talking on the phone. I don't talk to her all that often. I really only come home to sleep.

From when I was three until I was about fifteen, it was a very traumatic time. I suffered verbal and physical abuse and didn't feel as though I was truly loved by either of my parents.

I felt so alone, as though I wasn't worth talking to. I also became increasingly violent at school and was picked on for having such a bad temper.

Jess

Work with what you've already got. There is no point sitting around wishing you had a perfect family. There is no such thing. The best option is to try to sort out what is going on inside your family to the best of your ability.

Jess

MY PARENTS SHOULD HAVE SPLIT UP
BEFORE I WAS BORN

When I was two Dad actually left, then my parents got back together for me. Fifteen years of hell followed. There was constant arguing and it became so bad that Dad spent all his time working to avoid Mum, so I never saw him.

It hurt that Dad wasn't there for me. I was painfully aware that he wasn't around when I was growing up, and when I was eight I internalised my frustration and anger and withdrew.

As I got older, things got worse. I reached the stage where I didn't want anything for myself and quit everything, including my beloved sports and dance. I wasn't motivated to do anything at all. All I did was watch television.

This went on from Year 3 to Year 10. I struggled to make friends. I was brought up left to my own devices. I went to a Christian school where I was told I wasn't 'Christian' enough, and therefore not good enough. I only made one friend the whole time I was there. I started to believe that everybody hated me. Looking back I think this was a form of not coping, because I felt panicked and compelled to get out of there. I left in Year 8 and went to another school.

When I was in Year 10 I came across lewd text messages on my dad's phone from another woman. I was shocked and disillusioned. I had no idea what to do, so I kept it secret for three months. It all came out when Dad left emails between him and this woman on the home computer for Mum to see.

After that, everything went downhill. I didn't have a chance to feel anything because Mum had no-one and clung to me. I became her emotional crutch. She spent her days crying hysterically. I felt I couldn't say anything about Dad and I wasn't sure if I could even have a relationship with him.

My grief and sadness were overwhelming and the only way I could cope was to shut myself in my room and have no personal contact with anyone.

I pushed Mum away

I no longer have a relationship with my mother. After the divorce payout, she became obsessed with money. When I had trouble making ends meet, I needed her to help me sort out what to do, and she assumed I wanted money. My mum is a hard person to connect with on an emotional level, mostly because she believes she cannot hurt anyone and she is the only one who can be hurt. She tells me stories about Dad and tries to make me believe everything was his fault. Mum is a victim and blames everyone else for her predicament.

I have a stable relationship with my boyfriend and Mum can't handle that. She makes condescending remarks about it. I'm better at standing up to her now though. I told her I didn't want to have any contact with her until I get my feet on the ground. I miss her but I've got to get myself back on track. I took control of my life and set a boundary with Mum: 'This is what I need to do for myself right now and you need to respect that.'

It took a while for my self-esteem to build to the point where I could stand up to people, especially my mother. It's easier to be a victim but it feels horrible.

Alexis

I MISS MY MUM

My mum and I would spend the weekends together. I remember when I was really young running up to her whenever I heard her car. I missed her so much when I was growing up. I hated the fact I didn't live with her, hated the fact I didn't have a stable family.

I hid a lot of my pain from Mum. I was in a nutshell and whoever tried to crack me open would get a big hard smack across the face. Little things that usually wouldn't make me upset reduced me to tears. I started to get really violent and aggressive when I argued with anyone and back then I argued with anyone I could because I needed to vent. As much as I felt I was in control, it was obvious I was losing control.

My mother suffered issues which meant, by their nature, I couldn't live with her, so after my father died I lived with my grandparents. My mother cared so much for me; I was an angel in her eyes. I loved the fact she never held a grudge against me, no matter how loud I screamed, or what I said. But I found it really hard to open up to her because I didn't want her to be disappointed in me. I felt a sense of belonging that I'd been longing for, for such a long time, with Mum. It hurt that I couldn't be with her.

Veronica

I FELT LIKE NO-ONE CARED

I grew up knowing that Mum and Dad were doing drugs, and I was exposed to it on occasion. I felt abandoned from an early age, as though no-one really cared about me, and the drugs were more important than I was.

I remember, when I was five, running away from home and hiding in the local video store with my 3-year-old sister. Mum and Dad must have called the police because we could see police running around outside, but didn't know they were looking for us. Eventually we were found and taken home.

Another memory that haunts me from when I was five was my dad swinging a lounge chair around, yelling at me to stay back because he could see people at the front of our gate who were coming after us. But no-one was there. He was imagining it.

When I was seven, Mum decided to leave Dad and took me and my sister to another town. She said she did it for us and made a huge effort to get off the drugs. Eventually she succeeded.

Dad stayed in the city and continued to smoke pot. I only see him rarely, and on the occasions that I do, all he does is smoke pot in his room. I don't really have a relationship with him.

Mum works all the time so I've always been home alone and haven't had anyone to talk to or to be there for me after school.

I thought I was worthless

As a teenager I would cry all night and couldn't sleep until 3 a.m. I didn't know why at the time, but think it was because Mum was never there, and I convinced myself that nobody cared about me, that I was worthless.

Carrying all this pain and heartache around was like a brick in my stomach. It was always there and grew bigger and bigger until I couldn't take it anymore and broke down. I knew I wanted things to change but didn't know how to make it happen because I didn't trust many people and wouldn't speak to a counsellor.

I went to my first youth camp when I was sixteen. I was hurting so much inside. One of my friends had attended a Youth Insearch camp and asked me to come along as she thought it would help me.

At first I felt as though I didn't deserve to be at the camp because there were other teens with hardships worse than mine. This added to my feelings of worthlessness and I felt very vulnerable.

But I was made to feel safe and so I opened up and started talking about how I felt. It was such a freedom to talk about it after keeping it locked inside for so long.

Before the camp, I was too scared to let people in and didn't believe anyone when they said they cared about me. But at the camp I felt loved for the first time in forever. Nobody judged me and I was accepted for who I am, and people listened to me when I talked about my pain.

Emma

DAD'S BEEN DRINKING AGAIN

From the age of thirteen I have memories of my father physically abusing my mum. They had a very rocky relationship because my dad was an alcoholic with a gambling problem.

A few months after that my mum and dad split up, and my mum moved out and took me and my three brothers with her. I was happy that my parents split up because we could go to bed at night and not worry about hearing them fighting, and not be scared for our safety and our mum's safety anymore.

We moved to a new city eighteen months later to start fresh and so Mum could be closer to her family. My brothers and I started a new school and it was much bigger and more competitive than our previous school. My older brother attempted suicide about four months after we moved, which really hurt me because we were so close and he didn't talk to me before he tried to take his life. I know I could have helped him.

Soon after that I started hanging with the wrong crowds, and by the following year I was smoking, doing drugs, drinking alcohol and stealing. I got suspended twice and things at home were pretty tough. I had a few fights with my mum and brothers which turned violent. This made me feel very isolated and alone, and horrible on the inside.

Meg

I WAS COVERED IN BRUISES

When I was a baby, my parents used me to their advantage. They stole and hid things in my pram, and when they were caught they tried to claim it was me. I was only six months old.

I loved my grandmother because she always looked out for me. Once, she kidnapped me because she knew I was being bashed. No-one ever told me who hit me, why at times I was covered in bruises, or why my mother and father were the way they were.

My father left when I was really young and I don't remember much about it.

My mother found a new boyfriend. At first he seemed nice, everyone liked him, but it turned out he was sick in the mind. He sexually abused me when I was five.

My mother left him but didn't explain why. When I asked, she said she knew he'd done something bad but didn't want to tell anyone because she was scared no-one would believe her.

After this my mother couldn't cope, so I, along with my younger brother and two younger sisters, were cared for by a family friend for a while, who I became very close to. We still had access to our mother and would see her on occasion.

Then my mother met her new partner. He seemed a bit weird and creepy, even when he was smiling. He made me feel uneasy but I could never explain why, so I kept my feelings to myself.

When my mother decided she was ready for us to live with her again, the family friend refused. My grandmother intervened and we went to stay with her. But then my mother came over to my grandmother's house and demanded we go with her. The scene became ugly and my grandmother felt she had no other option than to let my mother take us.

I still remember the last words I said to my grandma: 'Don't cry Grandma, we'll be fine.' I was only six years old.

He caused my world to fall apart

One day soon after, my mother and her partner were asleep in bed and I had to get everyone ready for school. I tried to calm my siblings down by reading a book but one of my sisters was so bossy that she tried to make everything into a game. She ran halfway up the stairs and said, 'I'm the teacher'. I asked her to come back down, and eventually she did. But while this was going on, my baby sister had crawled all the way to the top of the stairs. My mother's partner had a collection of model aeroplanes and she had found them and was throwing them around. One of the pieces flew off. It could have easily been glued back on but my mother's partner didn't see it that way. In a blind rage he threw me up the stairs and across the carpet. I don't think he realised how strong he was. It was horrible and I was sobbing and felt a searing pain in my chin.

We ended up going to school that morning. I had no idea what I looked like and wondered why people kept asking if I was alright. Even my principal called me in and wanted to know what had happened. Later I found out my jaw had been dislocated, which shocked and upset me. I didn't understand how my mother's partner could be so violent with me when I was so much smaller than he was.

As I was walking home from school that day with my brother and sisters, two policemen pulled up and offered to take us home. But instead, they took us straight to the police station. I realised the school must have contacted them.

After that, we were taken to Grandma's house and stayed there for a month until we were split up and sent to foster care. I felt sad and confused. What had I done? It was scary.

All alone

I didn't like foster care. It wasn't so much the parents, more the other children who I didn't really get on with. The youngest child there was really mean; I once found him in a game of hide and seek, and he punched me in the stomach.

Eventually my sisters and brother moved back to the care of my mother, but I stayed in foster care. The authorities made me stay. Soon after, my mother ended up marrying her partner and I wasn't even invited to the wedding. I was so upset and I felt so lonely. Wasn't I important?

One day, about a month later, I was in after-school care and was asked where I'd like to spend Christmas. I said 'With my family', meaning my mother and siblings. They said, 'How about with your grandmother?' I was so excited because I hadn't seen my grandmother in a couple of months. I had to wait a week and when Grandma arrived to collect me, I was overjoyed. I ended up staying with my grandmother indefinitely after that, and for the first time in a long time, I felt I finally had a place I could call 'home'.

Jessica

DAD WAS A CONTROL FREAK

When I was baby, I lived with my mother, father and sister. There were complications during my birth and afterwards my mother was diagnosed with severe postnatal depression. It was later revealed that my mother actually has paranoid schizophrenia and severe depression, and doctors and psychotherapists believed she may have numerous other mental illnesses as well, including split personality disorder.

My parents had a rocky relationship as I was growing up. They both had major personal issues they were dealing with, which had to do with their own upbringings, while raising our family. It wasn't uncommon for me to live at home with my sister and only one parent, or even home alone without an adult.

Eventually my father separated from my mother. In an attempt to gain full custody of us, he claimed my mother was an 'unfit parent' and said she was 'dangerous to the health and wellbeing' of my sister and me (as well as herself). When this didn't work, he unlawfully abducted me and my sister to another state. I was only four years old at the time.

We only had the clothes on our backs, a small amount of money, huge debts and hardly any food. My father was a liar (among other things) and, as we grew up, he always said we had all these financial issues because my mother's adopted parents stole everything from us.

I'm yet to discover the real reason and I have learned there are always two sides to any story, but both my parents blamed the other and the truth is either buried or hidden.

From here things became worse and, as a result, by the age of sixteen I had moved about fourteen times, either renting with my father and sister, or moving from family member to family member. I never felt settled or had a sense of 'home' because I was moving around all the time.

Alyssa-Kate

ALL I EVER WANTED WAS A 'NORMAL' FAMILY

Sometimes I avoided sleeping over at my cousin's house or eating dinner with her family. It hurt to see them sit down at the table together and eat and talk about what happened in their day, like a normal family, because I never had this and knew I never would. Dinnertime in my house meant preparing whatever I could find in the cupboard and hoping it was edible.

At my aunty's house one time, there were two T-bone steaks and a few rissoles on offer and my uncle took one of the rissoles and left the steak for me and my cousin. I was like, 'Wow! An adult gave up a T-bone for a kid!'

Sometimes I'd be in the car when my aunt collected my cousin from school and I'd be amazed at how she was being picked up when she lived only one street away from the school. Then I'd watch my aunty give her a big hug and kiss as soon as she got into the car. My aunty would ask how her day had been and say how much she'd missed my cousin. When my cousin cut her arm, my aunty disinfected the cut, put a Band-aid on it and gave it a kiss to make it better. My cousin was ten years old and my aunty was still kissing her cut to make it better. It made me sad—that's something I've wished for all my life, to have a mother who loved and cared about me that way.

My aunty saw the way my brothers and I were treated as we were growing up and how badly it affected us, and I'm sure that's part of why she goes out of her way to be a loving and caring mum, and to make sure my cousin feels safe, nurtured and protected.

I truly believe that if more parents saw the hardships and neglect some of us go through as children, it would be a huge wake-up call and would change the way they treat their kids forever.

Jess

I felt like my dad didn't love me

It was my eleventh birthday and I opened up the present from my dad. It was socks and underwear. The underwear was a size 16. I'm a size 10. He then proceeded to give my brothers a Playstation game and new controller. They got better presents than I did and it was my birthday. As I cried in my room I was told I was ungrateful for my present, and my brothers teased me because they got a present on my birthday.

I've never been able to forget my eleventh birthday and how devastated my dad made me feel.

Sadly, I only have bad memories of times with my dad but I'm not bitter towards him. I'm more disappointed and hurt that he didn't show me the love I deserved as his daughter. But

I now realise that it's because of his issues not mine. You need to forgive others in order to move on and that's something that I have slowly done over the years.

Jess

TERRIFIED ABOUT ADOPTION

While growing up, I was recommended to the government child services agency for adoption as some of my school teachers suspected I wasn't living in sanitary or safe conditions at home. This happened from age six to thirteen; however, I was twelve when I was first kicked out of home.

I was a very hurt and angry little girl and I remember lashing out at my 'new parents' when they arrived at my high school to adopt me and take me away from my sister and my dad. I lived in denial for a short period of time, not wanting to believe that all that was happening to me was true. I still resent foster care agencies although I'm not sure why. I wish so much though that I could apologise to my foster care parents for hurting them and explain what I was going through so they'd understand why I treated them that way.

Alyssa-Kate

'PERFECT' LIFE STORIES

At school all the young girls loved their mums so much and their mothers would always tell them that they loved them. I wondered why my own mother never expressed these kinds of words or emotions. It made me feel as though I was missing out and I blamed myself because I thought it meant I wasn't good enough. I got angry at myself and thought I was the one who needed to change, to be perfect so she would notice.

In my group of friends, people would often share their life stories. It seemed everyone had perfect life stories and I convinced myself they must be lying. I always had good friends. Mum was so nice to my friends, and I wished she could be that nice to me. Everyone else's mum was nice to me, so I thought they must be mean to their children behind closed doors, because that's what my mum conditioned me to believe.

My idea of 'parents' and 'family' was so messed up.

Bronte

MUM ASKED ME TO LEAVE

I didn't cry for years. Because I withdrew and put a shell around myself, I wouldn't let my emotions get to that point. So when I finally let go I cried for hours. It felt so good. The trigger was the moment Mum turned on me and I felt all alone. We were fighting because I had to get to work and she wanted to have a talk and I didn't have time. She can't stand people walking away and she said, 'You're just like your father.' I replied, 'Say that one more time and I'm out of here.' Halfway through the day she sent me a message asking me to come and collect my things and leave. So I did. As soon as I drove away, I started crying. I went to my boyfriend's house and cried it all out. Although it was a horrible feeling, the sense of releasing all that pent-up emotion was enormous.

I like being emotional because I can feel. At the same time, the decision to disconnect from Mum for a while means I can grow in my own way. Perhaps down the track, in time, we will re-establish a healthier relationship.

Alexis

More information:
Family Services: www.nswfamilyservices.asn.au
Kids Matter: www.kidsmatter.edu.au
Kids Helpline: www.kidshelp.com.au Ph. 1800 55 1800
Lifeline: www.lifeline.org.au Ph. 13 11 14

An expert's view

1. Recognise that it is *not* your fault.
2. Share how you feel about it with someone you trust—a friend who has been through something similar, a trusted relative/sibling or teacher.
3. Try to stay focused on your own life and what brings you joy—sport, hobbies, friends, music, pets, etc.
4. Keep in contact with your friends and keep socialising with people who care about you.
5. Journal if it helps but try not to bottle it all up as it is very hard to get through this in silence and secrecy.
6. Call Kids Helpline on 1800 55 1800 or visit www.reachout. com.au or www.moodgym.asn.au for professional confidential anonymous support.
7. Inform yourself on what might happen next via familyrelationships.org.au or the Family Relationship

Advice Line on 1800 050 321 if you want more information on how custody and other practical/legal matters work.

8. If you can, be there to listen when your parents talk about what has happened but maintain boundaries around what you don't want to hear about. E.g. It's okay to say you don't want to hear one parent criticise or blame the other.

9. Try not to take sides; it takes two and your parents are likely to say hurtful things or react more than usual. Take it with a pinch of salt but again, maintain boundaries and tell them if you feel they are taking it out on you or pressuring you to take sides.

10. Work out what you want in terms of living arrangements and how much time you want to spend with each parent. This can take time and may change over time so keep talking to your parents and requesting adjustments until it works for you.

And again, recognise that it's *not* your fault.

Tessa Marshall

Director, Marshall Coaching Group

Have you heard of . . .

Marshall Coaching Group

www.marshallcoaching.com.au

Marshall Coaching Group can help you if you, or someone you know, is struggling with problems in their family, life, study or work.

In profile: Marcus

Age: 15

Hair colour: Blond/brown

Eye colour: Blue

Favourite saying: 'A penny saved is a penny earned' because if you do save money you can spend it on important things

Greatest personal moment: When I help out others or when someone compliments me

Dream yet to accomplish: To drive trains around Australia

Favourite colour: Blue

Favourite place in the world: Japan, because the people are awesome but different. Also the country has great scenery, great culture and landmarks.

Best tip: Believe in the positives in life, otherwise you'll just be stressing.

Favourite quote: 'That's one small step for man, one giant leap for mankind' because it was an amazing moment when man stepped on the moon; that big white thing that looks so far away in the night sky!

Dream for my future: To do well in school and do the best I can in my dream job of being a train driver

POWER STATEMENT
Always think positive.

If you live with one parent, you'll still be okay

'Love comforteth like sunshine after rain.'
William Shakespeare

It's hard when families break apart and you are left feeling alone, confused and often misplaced. You will probably feel as though there was something you could or should have done to stop it from happening. But the truth is, there is nothing you could have done. Parents split up often and when it happens it hurts. But it doesn't have to mean the end of the world. Of course it will feel shaky for a while. Give yourself time to get used to the way things are and know that life will settle down again before you know it.

I used to tell myself that I hated change and grit my teeth and wait impatiently for the feelings of discomfort to pass. Until I realised that change is inevitable. Everything is constantly changing and every experience helps us to grow and become more aware of ourselves and who we are.

Sometimes change can be the best possible result but it's hard to see this at the time, without the benefit of hindsight.

If you allow yourself time to adjust to the path of change, and talk to those you trust about your feelings and concerns, it will feel less scary.

Love is everything

Surround yourself with people who love you for who you are. People who encourage you to chase your dreams, emotionally support you as you work towards your goals, lift you up, inspire you, motivate you and celebrate your successes.

People like this enrich your life. They remind you in those moments of self-doubt that you deserve all that is good in life.

Love is universal. When we love others it brings us fulfilment. When someone loves us we feel worthy, valued and important.

Even if your childhood lacked love, you have the opportunity to change that by creating more love in your life and opening yourself up to those who love you now.

Be grateful for those close to you and be sure to tell them how much they mean to you. Show love by being kind and supportive, and a good listener.

And remember that if someone doesn't treat you with respect, or puts you down, you have every right to close them out of your life—but close them out with love.

Melinda

✍

It has been well established by research that in order to develop normally we need only one 'good enough' relationship with a parental figure. If you look around any school or community, you can see children who are doing very well, even thriving, who live in sole-parent households and there are many examples of highly successful individuals in public life who have grown up in sole-parent families. The quality of relationships in the child's life is more important than whether families have one parent or two.

Dianne Fitzjames

Clinical Psychologist, Team Leader
Adolescent Service, Prince of Wales Hospital

I NEVER GOT TO KNOW MY MUM OR SISTER

When I was seven years old, my mum disrespected my dad by sleeping with someone else. He gave her a couple of chances but eventually decided to divorce her. He went to court to seek custody of me and won. I ended up living with Dad, while my mum took my sister to another state.

Because of this I missed out on having a mother figure from a young age. I don't know my mum as well as I would like to and this makes me sad. There are times I wish the family wasn't split up. I don't know my sister at all and when I visited her and Mum recently, I found it hard to relate to my sister. We had a little bit in common, but I had trouble talking to her because I didn't know her very well. It made me feel even more alienated.

This situation created a hole in my life that, for the longest time, I couldn't seem to fill. I had days of intense loneliness. It was really hard and I felt misunderstood and depressed.

Because I don't see them much and we only talk a few times a year, it's been hard to build a relationship. I realise how much I miss them when I see them, and how different my life would have been if I'd grown up in a family environment.

I can't change what happened, I can only learn to deal with it the best way I can. Dad loves me and he's a good father. I've stopped wishing my situation was different, and I'm learning to live with it and accept it. I'm not allowing it to dictate who I am or what my self-worth is.

Sharing my feelings with other people in similar situations helped me a lot. I found a loving and nurturing environment on the youth camps I attended and this helped me to feel more complete as a person. I also made a lot of new friends.

If you live with one parent

My advice to anyone in the same situation is to get close to the parent you live with. Be open with them. Tell them how you feel and seek support. As long as you feel loved, you will feel worthwhile. And if you don't, go where you know there is love—a relative or close friends. Talk to your friends about how you're feeling and lean on them for support to get you through the tough times.

Marcus

Advice for single parents
- Support your child when they're down.
- Make sure they know that they are loved, and that they feel it.
- Listening to your child is so important because this makes them feel valued.

Marcus

There's no reason you can't make a success of your life

Growing up in a single-parent household doesn't mean you're going to be a failure or a damaged human being. The reason why single-parent households attract such negative attention is that they often experience more difficulties than households with both a mum and a dad. These hardships range from lack of money to the absence of a male or female role model.

Where these difficulties are present, they can be tough to overcome, but are far from insurmountable. If you are in that situation, it helps to seek out people to help you, like relatives or close friends, or check out local youth programs and organisations you can get involved with.

Another important thing to note is that not all single-parent households are problem households. Many single parents are extremely capable people who are able to provide all the love, discipline and support you need. While the make-up of your family may differ from those of other teens, it still represents your family unit.

Also, what is important is that you are happy in your environment. If you're unhappy or feel something is missing, you should talk to the people you trust about how you're feeling, and what you can do to make changes or adjustments so that you feel safe and secure.

I grew up with Mum and nine siblings. We were dearly loved but didn't have much money. There was one dad who stayed a while and became involved with us, but I didn't relate to him, so I didn't have a male role model in the home. The housework and stress of ten children would get on top of Mum, so I often went without the basics—like clean clothes or good meals. The house was normally messy too. Our home environment often frustrated and angered me. I think in some ways it hampered my success at school and in other areas. I didn't miss having a dad all that much, because Mum and I found replacement male role models for me outside of the home; people I bonded with and came to trust, who became very important in my life. Mum's love sustained me, and the male role models guided my development as a young boy, such as by providing discipline. But I think I would have struggled to succeed and be happy if I wasn't taught by a program called Youth InSearch that I was worthwhile despite my environment, and that my environment would not determine who I was to become; only I would.

Youth InSearch also brought me into contact with other young people in a similar situation. It felt reassuring to know I wasn't the only one growing up with one biological parent.

Drawing on these revelations, I decided to make a success of my life despite my circumstances, and am now a lawyer in one of Australia's top law firms. I am happy in life and know that whatever decisions I choose to make for myself, if I apply the same determination, confidence and faith in myself as I always have, it will lead to fulfilment.

We all have control over our futures. As individuals, we determine the path we take; success is not dictated by our circumstances.

Heath Ducker
Lawyer and author of A Room at the Top

DOES GROWING UP WITH ONE PARENT MEAN I'M DISADVANTAGED?

As long as you have positive male and female role models, you'll be fine. Support from grandparents, aunts, uncles or close family friends means you will have the benefit of having those extended family members as role models.

Beth

Choice determines the path we decide to take in life. We are all born into different circumstances and it is up to us to make a success of our lives.

Molly

Growing up in a single-parent family has made me a stronger person. When Mum needed something done around the house, she didn't sit around feeling sorry for herself, she just got on with it. Because I learned to be independent from a young age, I'm very much the same and I love that about myself.

Callum

It seems wrong to assume that someone who doesn't grow up with a mum and dad at home is going to have a more difficult life. Some parents choose to stay together 'for the children' and are always unhappy. Living in this kind of environment is not better than living with one stable, happy and loving parent. I grew up with just my mum and sister and we turned out fine.

Hannah

Single-parent households can be just as strong as two-parent households. People from all walks of life can turn out in many different ways. I grew up in a single-parent household and had a great childhood. I don't believe it's right to judge people for the family they grow up in. Two-parent households have their problems too.

Ben

I grew up in a single-parent home and started drinking, doing drugs and having sex before I was even a teenager. I have since straightened out my life, but can't help but wonder how much worse I would have turned out if I'd grown up watching Mum suffer every day of her life if she'd stayed with Dad. Because of what Mum's been through, I would never stay trapped inside an unhappy relationship because there are children. I don't want a child of mine growing up thinking that it's normal to be miserable in a relationship.

Madison

I'm more successful because I came from a single-parent home. I'm a doctor and proud of how far I've come. Because of my circumstances, I learned to take care of myself at a young age and be independent, and this has helped me tackle many of life's challenges.

Joey

I know my mum would've loved for me to grow up with two parents who loved each other, but that simply hasn't happened. Mum has done her best to make the most of what some would consider a tough situation. I have a really close relationship with my mum and don't for a second believe I am disadvantaged in any way. In fact I feel really lucky.

Saskia

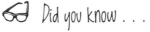 Did you know . . .
Several studies have indicated that it is increasingly clear that family processes (e.g. inter-parental relationships, parenting practices), as opposed to structure (e.g. number, gender or sexuality of parents), contribute to determining a child's current and future wellbeing.[3]

Chapter 3

YOU'RE NOT ALONE

If you're feeling lost, it may comfort you to know that you're not alone. Everyone experiences times of darkness at some point in their life, some longer than others, some more frequently than others and some blacker than others.

It might be a result of the loss of a loved one, the loss of innocence, a result of abuse, neglect or the absence of a stable family unit. It might be none of those, yet alone you still feel the pain. Find someone who you trust and talk to them about how you are feeling. It is important to seek out a person who you feel you can wholeheartedly trust with your deepest fears, feelings and needs. When you know that you can trust and rely on this person, enlist their support and allow them to help you seek what it is that you need most.

In profile: Jess

Age: 16

Hair colour: Brown

Eye colour: Hazel/olive

Favourite saying: 'LOL'

Greatest personal moment: Being accepted into leader's training at Youth Insearch

Dream yet to accomplish: Travel to Russia

Favourite colour: Blue

Favourite place in the world: Russia—they have the best food

Best tip: Don't let life's disappointments get you down.

Favourite quote: 'Even if you're on the right track, you'll get run over if you just sit there.' *Will Rogers*

Dream for my future: To have a happy, healthy family

POWER STATEMENT

Find a way to deal with it and then get over it.

Have you heard of . . .

Kids Helpline

Phone 1800 55 1800

www.kidshelp.com.au

Kids Helpline is Australia's only free, private and confidential telephone and online counselling service specifically for young people aged between five and 25 years old.

You'll talk directly with a counsellor when you call Kids Helpline. Each time you call:

- You will hear a recorded message that tells you about how Kids Helpline works.
- After listening to this message, you will be connected with a counsellor.
- When you call, you can choose to speak to either a male or female counsellor. You don't have to say your name and what you talk about is just between you and your counsellor.
- The counsellor you speak to will tell you his or her name, so if you call again, you can ask to speak to the same person.
- Your counsellor will ask you what you would like to talk about and ask you some questions to help understand what's going on for you.
- You can talk to us for as long as you like. Email and web counselling is also available.

We can support you by:

- listening to and understanding things from your point of view
- talking with you about what has been happening and how you think or feel about it
- helping you to figure out some ideas of how you might be able to handle things
- helping you decide what to do
- providing you with information and support to find other services that can help.

What is your personal message to young people facing hardship?

Every person experiences hardship at some point in their life, and young people often face difficulties that they don't yet have the experience to handle well. My message to any young person facing hardship is to reach out to other people and share your concerns. While it is great to have friends to rely on, there will be times when you need to talk to people with greater life experience, and maybe specialist skills, who may well have some options for what to do about the problem.

If there is a problem in your life that you are struggling with, then seek support from Kids Helpline, we're waiting to listen to you. Call 1800 55 1800.

In profile: Jasmin

Age: 17

Hair colour: Blonde

Eye colour: Grey

Favourite saying: 'Do or do not. There is no try.'

Dream yet to accomplish: Travel to Europe

Favourite colour: Yellow

Favourite place in the world: Wilsons Promontory, it's so beautiful, and my dad liked it there too

Best tip: Good things come to those who wait, and great things are worth waiting for.

Favourite quote: 'Be the change you wish to see in the world.' *Gandhi*

Dream for my future: To become a youth worker

POWER STATEMENT

I know it's really hard, but you've got to stay positive and think positive. Believe in yourself, because to be happy you have to accept yourself first before others will accept you. And if you don't like something, change it.

Q: HOW CAN I PERSUADE MY TROUBLED FRIEND TO SEEK HELP?

A: If you are concerned for the wellbeing of a friend, encourage them to reach out for help from a supportive adult such as a family member, a teacher that they respect at school, or a counsellor at Kids Helpline.

If the troubled friend is reluctant to seek help, then it may be useful to offer to support them in making the initial contact. Go with them to a meeting or be with them during the first phone call. If you're not sure how to support a friend, then the best thing to do is ask a question like, 'What can I do to make it easier for you to talk to _____?'

If you're concerned that your friend is likely to seriously harm themselves, then the most important thing is to pass on your concerns immediately to a responsible adult. This is not 'dobbing' or betraying the friendship, it is taking an important step to get the help to ensure the safety of a friend in real distress.

Wendy Protheroe

General Manager Counselling Services, Kids Helpline

Sometimes writing things down can help you to understand exactly what it is that is troubling you most. Start a journal and don't be afraid to write everything in it. Getting in touch with how you are feeling can often help clarify what the problem is and how to work

Reassure them that while you might not understand or have experienced how they are feeling, you will be a good listener and not judge them. In saying that, I believe that you can bring a horse to water but you can't make them drink. The troubled friend really needs to want help in the first place and be open to have someone assist them. There are many wonderful organisations and youth services available to provide assistance. Support your friend by encouraging them to talk to someone who is in a position to help (or to at least find help); like, a teacher/school counsellor, GP or family friend.

Jessica Brown

CEO & Founder, Life Changing Experiences Foundation

- Let your friend know that you're there to listen to them and help as a friend but it's the best idea to talk to someone who is trained.
- Don't underestimate the power and importance of listening—there is a lot of pressure to 'fix' problems as a

friend but listening is a fantastic way to make your friend feel connected and accepted.

- Give your friend some information that they can read in their own time—you may like to download/share some info from the reachout.com.au website.
- Encourage them to explore the different ways to seek help as some people may feel uncomfortable speaking to someone face to face initially. There are many anonymous online and phone services (state and national) that offer advice, guidance and counselling.
- Let your friend know that they are not 'different' or 'weird' or 'weak' to seek help—that in fact it takes strength to seek help. Congratulate + encourage them and make them feel good about seeking help.

Charlotte Beaumont-Field
Wellbeing Manager, Inspire Foundation

Listen, really listen. Don't offer advice or tell them what to do. Acknowledge the pain they are in. Allow them to tell you their reasons for wanting to die or for their unhappiness. Don't offer clichés or say it will be alright.

Then, once you think they have really felt heard by you without judgement or advice-giving, tentatively explore options. Ask them what they see as their options, what would they like to do. Ask, if this was their friend, what advice they would give that friend.

Most people come up with the idea of seeking help themselves but if they don't, you could raise it by suggesting, 'I care for you and am worried about you. No-one should have to go through this alone and a professional could really help you. How do you feel about getting some professional help? What if I make the appointment for you? How about if I go with you?' Perhaps share any knowledge you have of how others have been helped.

But don't push them or force them.

Then check-in regularly with them and also ensure you look after your own health and wellbeing.

The exception is where you fear that they are suicidal. Ask if they are having suicidal thoughts and if they are, get further help yourself to ensure they are getting the help they need. You may need to tell their parents or get help from a school teacher or counsellor even if it means breaching trust. Where there is risk of suicide, your duty of care over-rides your duty of trust. Better to have your friend alive and angry at you than living with the inevitable 'what ifs' that occur if they take their life and you are left wondering what else you could have done.

Tessa Marshall

Director, Marshall Coaching Group

In profile: Emma

Age: 18
Hair colour: Sandy blonde
Eye colour: Brown
Favourite saying: 'Keep smiling.'
Greatest personal moment: When I can get someone to smile when they feel down about themselves
Dream yet to accomplish: Swim with turtles
Favourite colour: Green, aqua
Favourite place in the world: In the surf on my bodyboard
Best tip: Smile for one second and in that second you feel a hundred times better.
Favourite quote: Breathe life—have faith.
Dream for my future: To continue supporting young people going through a hard time and seeing them smile

POWER STATEMENT

I learned that I don't have to conform to what everyone else believes I should or shouldn't be doing. It doesn't matter how other people feel about what I'm doing, what matters is how I feel.

Chapter 4

ABUSE—IT'S NOT OKAY

'Never bend your head. Hold it high. Look the world straight in the eye.'
Helen Keller

Just because someone decides they are going to treat you a certain way doesn't mean it's okay. Any form of abuse—emotional, physical or sexual—is most definitely not okay. Sometimes abuse can be out of your control. You were too young to know what was happening, too shocked to react or you tried to tell someone but they didn't believe you. You may have even been threatened that if you told anyone, something worse would happen to you or someone you love.

Most of what happens to us when we are growing up is out of our direct control. And abuse is one of the worst acts someone in a position of trust or authority can inflict upon an innocent person. Those who abuse are the only ones who should feel guilty or ashamed.

If you are a victim of abuse, you are a *victim*. Although it feels horrible, remember that you are innocent. You have not done anything wrong, and you are not a bad person.

Abuse can leave you feeling angry, even enraged. It can help to express these feelings in a constructive way. Let yourself feel whatever emotions come to the surface and make sure you talk it out as often as you need to with someone you trust. There is plenty of support available to help you get back on track.

Coping with sexual abuse

An incident of sexual abuse can turn your world upside down. It can leave you feeling scared, worthless, hopeless and you can even feel as though it was somehow your fault. Even if the person who abused you threatens violence if you dare breathe a word to anyone, keeping it bottled up will only cause further pain and distress.

An act of sexual abuse is a crime. It is not okay for anyone to take advantage of you in this way. If you are a victim of sexual abuse, tell someone you trust as soon as possible. Help is always there if you need it.

Melinda

I WAS ABUSED BY MY FATHER'S 'FRIEND'

I was sexually abused by a neighbour almost every day for more than a year when I was ten years old. He was one of my father's friends and I was too scared to tell anyone. He would bribe me with presents and act as if it was normal to keep 'our little secret' safe. I suppressed it until I was seventeen, when finally I had to break my silence and tell someone. I told a person who was really close to me who was involved with a program called SISTER2sister which I was a part of.

When it came out I felt scared because my feelings became unpredictable. I didn't trust any male and withdrew into myself. I suffered through flashbacks for the next year, and continued to remember certain things about what had happened that I had pushed so far into the back of my mind I'd forgotten them. I also suffered feelings of worthlessness and major guilt for what had happened to me; I believed it was my fault.

My mother blamed herself, and my father told me to 'get over it'.

Last I heard the perpetrator went to jail for physically abusing a relative of his and committed suicide. At least now, I don't have to look over my shoulder.

Lauren

I WAS ONLY SIX YEARS OLD

One of the neighbours in our street molested me when I was six. I knew what was happening was wrong but I was too embarrassed to tell anyone. I started slacking off at school. I swore at the teachers and started fights because I was so messed up inside. It wasn't until I was twelve that I opened up to my best friend and told her about what had happened. I felt better for talking about it, but the incident still haunted me.

Justin

NO-ONE BELIEVED ME

I constantly had flashbacks of incidents with my father. I didn't even know what was happening to me until someone explained what flashbacks were. I told my mum and my sister about my father's sexual abuse, but they didn't believe me. My father denied it.

Amy

MY FRIEND'S BOYFRIEND RAPED ME

I made friends with a girl three years older than me who lived around the corner, and started hanging out with her. One night I went around there and she was with her boyfriend, who was much older. I got drunk and he took advantage of me and raped me. I was so scared and ashamed, I didn't tell anyone for ages.

What made it worse was my mother accused me of doing all these things I hadn't been doing. One night, she started screaming at me and violently whipped me with a belt. I had nasty red marks all over my arms that stung like hell and I couldn't stop crying.

I didn't want to go back to Mum after that. The community service department took me and placed me in foster care.

After the first week in foster care, I had a pregnancy scare from the rape. I was late, my breasts were swollen and I had unexplainable morning sickness. I was in an unfamiliar place, all alone, but with courage and support from friends, I confided in a school counsellor who helped me. The test was negative and I felt so relieved, like someone was watching over me. Police investigators had to interview me. I sat in a room with an obtrusive camera recording me, and two men asking me personal questions about the sexual act. It was horrible and uncomfortable. I decided not to press charges, because I felt as though it was my fault.

At the first foster care home, there was a mother and her 18-year-old daughter, and two little foster boys. The mother and daughter were horrible to me. I wasn't allowed out of the house. The mother wouldn't let me see my brothers unless I made an arranged time. The one time I tried, she insisted on giving me cleaning chores so I couldn't get out to see them.

So I ran away.

I spent a week living with my brothers and rebelling. I pierced my nose and barely ate until eventually the community service department agreed to let me live with another lady who I adored, saw what I was going through and wanted to adopt me, and since then I haven't looked back.

I learned from the rape to respect myself more and that I shouldn't put myself in unsafe situations. I realised that I wasn't as old as I kept trying to be and that even though I depended on myself, I needed someone who was there for me.

Natashia

HE SAID HE'D KILL ME IF I SAID ANYTHING

When I was eleven my best friend and I were both raped by her older brother when we were in the shower when I stayed over there one night. I didn't tell my mum until a few months after. I was scared that he would kill me because he threatened me with a pocket knife. Eventually I told my mum because

I didn't understand what happened at the time and I feared I was pregnant.

When I was fourteen my mum let me stay with friends while she went away. That night, when everyone had gone to bed, my friend's dad came into the room and tried to rape me. I screamed at him to leave me alone and eventually he did. I felt very shaken up by that incident. I went home early the next morning and told my brother what happened. I didn't want anyone else to know because of all the things I'd already been through when I was eleven. But the next day my brother went to the police and told them and they rang my mum and she organised an interview with the police.

I decided to press charges because I'd heard some stories about how dangerous my friend's father could be, and I knew that by pressing charges I could help to make it safer for my friend and her family.

Meg

I WASN'T ALLOWED TO SLEEP OVER

My mum was sexually abused as a child. Until I was a teenager and she could make me aware of the dangers, she wouldn't let me sleep over at my friends' houses if they had brothers or if their father lived in the house.

Kerry

MY DAD SHOULD BE IN GAOL

My father's girlfriend hated me. She constantly put me down, calling me ugly and making mean comments about my weight because I was a chubby kid. She even threatened me when nobody else was around. They later broke up and Dad told me that he didn't particularly like her for his own reasons but wanted to stay with her so my sister and I would have a 'mother figure'. I confided how she treated me and Dad broke down in tears. Seeing him in pain made me feel vindicated at first, but then I felt guilty because I'd secretly hoped they'd break up.

Dad's second girlfriend (now my stepmother) was horrid to me. Just like the previous girlfriend, she resented me due to the fact that Dad was so fond of me and referred to me as 'Daddy's little girl'. But also because he 'affectionately touched' me. When she discovered (early in their relationship) that my dad was molesting me, she ignored it and didn't even try to intervene. She still to this day denies my father's actions. It makes me feel sick to my stomach.

As well as physical and emotional abuse, Dad sexually abused me from when I was about seven years old. During a holiday with my mother and stepfather, they explained some illegal activities that my father had either taken part in, or was still involved in, such as using drugs. I started to become more aware and understood that what he was doing was wrong.

My father and I don't talk anymore. Since I left to move back with my mother, we spoke every six months but the conversations became too awkward and after hanging up I'd run to my room and burst into tears.

I still to this day hold fear for the two little girls left in the house with my father, as they are both in the age group of when my sexual abuse occurred. Police investigations commenced, instigated by the authorities, my counsellor and other people looking out for me and my sister's wellbeing. But the only witnesses for my sister and I were too scared to come forward, so after a short investigation they couldn't produce enough leads to continue or to sentence my father.

I felt mixed emotions that my father may have faced sentencing because of the abuse. I still love my father and have forgiven him for his actions and the person he became due to a concoction of drugs, alcohol, hatred and violence, as even to this day I would like to think that with a little help the person underneath could one day shine through again. I'm not sure.

Alyssa-Kate

More information
Rosie's Place: a community-based sexual assault counselling service for children, young people and their non-offending family members
www.rosiesplace.com.au/contact.html
Rape Crisis Centre: www.nswrapecrisis.com.au
Violence Against Women (VAW): www.lawlink.nsw.gov.au

What if I'm being physically or emotionally abused?

Physical or emotional abuse is the act of overpowering or controlling someone through humiliation, manipulation and fear. It disarms confidence, causes anxiety and chips away at a person's self-esteem.

While an act of physical abuse involves actual physical harm, emotional abuse happens when someone is constantly criticised, insulted or belittled.

People who are physically and/or emotionally abused feel like isolating themselves out of fear and often feel uneasy around other people. This can create a longing for love and approval which can lead to a desperate desire to please others and to be liked.

Victims of ongoing physical or emotional abuse become convinced they are worthless and sometimes the idea of seeking help can feel too overwhelming. It is important to remember that help is there if you need it and taking control of the situation by asking for help is a positive first step towards regaining your confidence.

Melinda

MY STEPFATHER CONSTANTLY TAUNTED ME

After Dad left we moved into my grandparents' place for a couple of years. Then Mum met a guy who lived with us for twelve years. He took an instant dislike to me and, as it turned out, was an extremely violent person. I was nine when he started verbally taunting me and eleven when he started hitting me. He was a strong guy, and although I was a reasonable size too, he had it over me mentally. I grew afraid of him and mentally recoiled when he physically abused me. He threatened that if I told Mum or anyone else, he'd kill me. The blend of emotional and physical abuse was difficult and the atmosphere at home was tense during my teenage years.

Sometimes Mum would jump to my defence, but this would result in both Mum and me fighting him off and then complete chaos would ensue and he'd become violent with objects. One time he ripped the phone cord out of the wall.

A number of times Mum insisted that he left, but he always managed to convince her to take him back. On those occasions, Mum would justify it by telling me, 'You can't necessarily change him but you can change your approach to him.'

The abuse affected me to the point where I started flunking school. I was also drawn into unhealthy relationships and friendships. I think the experiences at home knocked my confidence around and that affected me.

The worst part was, as a result of being physically and emotionally abused, I didn't like myself. Sadness and depression often overwhelmed me and I struggled with feelings of worthlessness.

Tom

MUM TOOK HER ABUSIVE CHILDHOOD OUT ON ME

When I was ten, Mum's father died. She'd made no secret of the fact that she believed her father loved me more than he loved her. She took his death particularly hard and closed off from the family, spending most days locked away in her room.

Mum stopped communicating with me altogether. I only had Dad and my brothers to talk to now and started to feel as though only males would listen to me. I took on the belief that females didn't like me because I was female.

Mum had a really unhappy childhood with an abusive father and a mother who cowered and did what she was told. I'm sure that's why she hit me. Sometimes she would wake me up at night just because she was awake, or stand at my door and flick on and off my lights to get my attention. I thought she was trying to torment me, but looking back I think she didn't know what to do or how to say, 'I'm bored so I need you to talk to me' or 'I need you to help me with the washing'.

Bronte

MUM'S BOYFRIENDS WERE MORE IMPORTANT THAN ME

Mum always put her boyfriends before me. She physically abused me as well. There were times she'd belt me with a broom while I cowered, hands shielding my body.

On my sixth birthday I woke up to find my mother having sex with a strange man. My mother didn't have any respect for the fact that I was sleeping in the same room as her. Around this time, I developed suicidal feelings.

Natashia

MUM TOLD THE POLICE I'D BEEN KIDNAPPED

My big brother does shift work with my stepdad so they are not around much and only come home to sleep. My little brother stays at friends' houses for the same reasons I do. We all get that the more we stay away from Mum, the more peace we will have.

One time, I didn't tell Mum where I was going and she called the police and told them I'd run away from home. They told her that because I was sixteen I had the right to go wherever I wanted. Then she rang back and said I'd been kidnapped so they'd do something. The police asked for my mobile number and they left a message on my phone saying my mother had said I'd been kidnapped and that if it was a false accusation to please call back. I was like, 'What the hell?' I called them back and told them I'd run away from home. I went to my aunt's house and she called Mum and told her I was staying there. My mum was furious with my aunty for letting me stay with her but she realised it was better for me to stay there than on the streets.

Jess

I WATCHED DAD BEAT MY SISTER

My sister and I were both physically abused by my father. However, he either denied it or explained it away as 'punishment'. He often said it was 'acceptable' to hurt us to teach us a lesson and that it wasn't 'as bad' as we made it out to be, nor was it 'illegal'.

I still remember the time my sister was young and she did something wrong and to 'punish her' Dad snapped a few wooden spoons and a metal one in half across her bottom. She was in such excruciating pain that every time she had to move she would gingerly take care, wincing and whimpering. She couldn't sit down on her bottom properly without screaming in pain for about three or four weeks. Her bottom was blackened; covered in bruises and welts. This made me feel helpless—all I could do was be 'weak' and give in to standing there watching, frozen to the spot, hearing the screams and pleas of my sister with every smack across her bottom, seeing the pain screw up her pretty face and feel her pain as if it was my own.

When he hit me, I threw my hands up and cowered behind them, wincing with every smack, trying to escape. I scrunched my eyes closed and searched deep down in my heart for that 'special place' where no-one or nothing could hurt me. That was my only defence with my father. The way I saw it, he could hurt me physically, emotionally and psychologically to his heart's content, but he could never hurt my spirit—my soul.

Alyssa-Kate

More information
Kids Helpline: www.kidshelp.com.au
Phone 1800 55 1800
Lifeline: www.lifeline.org.au Phone 13 11 14
Education Centre Against Violence (ECAV):
www.ecav.health.nsw.gov.au

An expert's view

- Know that this situation is not your fault—it is NEVER okay to experience any form of abuse—no matter what.
- You may get told that you 'deserve' the treatment or that your behaviour caused them to treat you this way—this is NOT true.

- You may experience many emotions—you may feel guilty, frightened, confused, alone and helpless.
- The best thing to do is to get some help—calling Kids Helpline on 1800 55 1800 or using their web and email counselling service through their website www.kidshelp.com.au is a good place to start.
- Do not keep quiet—even if the person who is abusing you tells you not to tell anyone, you need to tell someone, preferably an adult or someone older than you. Maybe there is a teacher at school, another parent or a school counsellor you feel comfortable talking to? If so, please let them know what you are feeling. Write it down and give them the note if you feel uncomfortable talking to them face to face.
- There is help out there and people who want to help you— you are not alone.
- It can be scary, but calling the police—especially if you are at risk of immediate harm—is a good thing to do.

Charlotte Beaumont-Field

Wellbeing Manager, Inspire Foundation

In profile: Meg

Age: 15

Hair colour: Brown

Eye colour: Brown

Favourite saying: 'Mad'

Greatest personal moment: A recent celebration dinner when I got up and spoke to people about myself and they really wanted to listen to me

Dream yet to accomplish: Becoming a leader for Youth Insearch or finishing school and going to university to study to become a journalist or indigenous health worker

Favourite colour: Purple

Favourite place in the world: My dad's house because it was built by my ancestors and it has been passed on through the family so it has a safe vibe around it

Best tip: You can't be helped unless you want to be helped. Think outside the square.

Favourite quote: 'Footsteps in the sands of time were never made sitting down.' *Anonymous*

Dream for my future: To be a journalist on a national current affairs program

Chapter 5

LIVING WITH AN ALCOHOLIC PARENT

Living with an alcoholic parent means you don't even feel safe in your own home. Your stability feels threatened and you may feel 'on guard' to protect your safety, perhaps even the safety of your siblings.

Your wellbeing is important, so if you are in danger the best thing you can do for yourself is to make sure there is an alternative—a relative who can take you in, even if it's only temporary, or a friend's place nearby where you can go if things become ugly at home. You might feel guilty for leaving your parents and unsettled by the thought that you don't feel safe in your own home, but remember that this is not your fault. You did not create the situation and by taking action to protect yourself and preserve your own wellbeing, you are letting your parents know that their behaviour is not okay.

Finding support

Change is inevitable and often comes when we stand up for ourselves. There are people who are there to help and support you so don't be afraid to ask for help, and never feel ashamed of your situation. You deserve to be in an environment where your safety is not compromised.

Melinda

I WAS SO ANGRY WITH MUM I HIT HER

My dad died of a drug overdose when I was eleven. I felt so sad. I didn't get to know my dad as well as I'd hoped and never would. And I was stuck with an alcoholic mother.

For so long, when I missed my dad, when I felt alone and sad, I yearned for my mother to be there, to listen and talk, and to understand what I was going through.

But because of her drinking, I never got the love and nurturing from Mum that I needed to cope with the grief I felt over Dad's death. I became upset and watching her get drunk and lie around all day began to frustrate me.

I started to get very angry; at my dad for leaving me, but mostly at my mother for being selfish and neglecting me and my sister when we were going through pain and heartache trying to make sense of life without Dad.

My anger became so bad that I punched holes in the wall to cope with the overwhelming rage that often consumed me.

Then it got out of control, to the point where I started physically abusing my mother. She didn't think she had a problem and this was extremely frustrating to me because whenever I tried to talk to her about her drinking and how badly it was affecting my sister and me, she'd tell me I was wrong.

I became scared. I didn't recognise myself when I was in a blind rage and once the anger started to build I couldn't seem to control it.

I knew it was wrong to get that angry to the point of absolute rage where I'd lash out physically at my mother. I felt ashamed, but at the same time I didn't know how else to handle the overwhelming emotions I was feeling, coupled with the lack of support or care from her.

My older sister is amazing; she is like a real mum to me. She cooks dinner and does everything for me that Mum should do, but doesn't. My sister helped me reach the decision to talk to a counsellor about how I was feeling.

What should you do?

If your mum or dad is an alcoholic or drug addict, talk to someone external to family—a trusted relative or counsellor. Don't let anger build up.

Daniel

MY MOTHER AND STEPFATHER DRANK CONSTANTLY

I was a victim of physical abuse due to alcohol. My mother and stepfather were always in a drunken state. It wasn't unusual for my stepfather to push me and hit me when he was drunk, if he thought I was being disobedient (even when I was on my best behaviour).

I was secretly afraid of him for a long time.

When I discovered my stepfather was overdosing on my mum's medication, I became even more afraid of what he might do. I told him to stop and he yelled at me and hit me really hard across the back. Mum slapped him across the face and then he started laying into her. I couldn't believe it—I was crying hysterically because I'd never seen Mum being beaten up before, and by someone in our family who we trusted, all because he was drunk. It was horrible to hear Mum's sobs and watch her cowering in fear as he repeatedly bashed her. My brother was there but he pretended not to notice and sat watching the television. I think he feared my stepfather too.

I felt so helpless, and didn't know what to do, so I called the police and they came and took my stepfather away. I felt so guilty. He had to spend the night in a cell. The one positive thing was that because Mum became an unwilling victim of the violence brought on by my stepfather's alcohol abuse, it was a wake-up call for her and everyone in my family.

With my stepfather out of the house, I confided to my mum how badly her drinking affected me, and how distraught I'd become being around my stepfather, to the point where I was terrified to be in the same room as him.

After that incident, my mum stopped drinking and asked my stepfather to stop as well.

Mum says she'll never drink again. Even junk mail offering discount alcohol at the local store makes her feel sick. She constantly tells me she loves me. I think she feels guilty for everything I've been through as a result of her alcohol abuse.

I know she loves me but I feel really hurt that she let it go that far before she took action to stop it.

What should you do?

If your parents are drinking and becoming physically abusive, tell them you don't like it and will not tolerate it. Remove yourself from the situation by going to a friend's house or into another room (and locking the door if necessary). If they continue to behave this way, tell a relative or close family friend, and have them intervene to help you. Get support outside your family. Organisations like Youth Insearch, where you are surrounded by people who have been through what you are going through and can give you advice and support, can really help you.

Kerry

MUM'S DRUNK AGAIN

My mum is an alcoholic and smokes a packet of cigarettes a day. My mum and stepdad fight constantly. There is conflict in almost everything they do. Mum doesn't have a job, my stepdad has three, she smokes, he hates smoking, she drinks and he doesn't. It gets really stressful as often I want to take my stepdad's side because I know he's right in what he says, but Mum is my flesh and blood. So instead I try to stay neutral.

I'm grateful I have my ex-boyfriend, because although we've broken up, we're still good friends. The other week Mum and I were having a terrible argument and my ex had to pull us apart. I know I can call on him for help and support any time, and his friends have been amazing too. They can see what a difficult home life I have, and at times they have driven by and picked me up to get me out of the house when Mum is on one of her drunken rampages.

In my own personal experience, once 5 p.m. hits it is time to get out of house, or get into your bedroom and lock the door. Otherwise someone will barge into your room and yell at you and abuse you over nothing.

On thin ice

Sometimes my mother has called me when she's drunk and abused me over the phone. At least with a phone call you can hang up. When someone barges into your room, there is nowhere to go.

> I always have a spare shirt, underwear and pants in my bag because I don't know when I'm going to need to stay at friend's house if something happens at home.
> Jess

What should you do?

Have a safe place where you can go anytime—the home of a trusted friend or relative—that is close enough to get to in a hurry but not close enough that a drunken parent can stumble there. Make sure your parents know you're safe so they don't call the police. They need to have peace of mind that you're safe and then they can sort out their issues. The worst thing you can do is to take off and not let your parents know where you are, as the police get called and it turns into a big ugly battle which then has to be documented and a report filed.

Jess

More information
Kids Helpline: Phone 1800 55 1800
www.kidshelp.com.au
Lifeline: Phone 13 11 14 www.lifeline.org.au
SANE Helpline: Phone 1800 18 SANE (7263) www.sane.
org/youth/youth/helping_young_people_understand_
mental_illness.html

What to do if your parents are alcoholics

- If your parents are drinking too much, it affects you in many ways—you could have to take on more responsibilities around the house, you may have to put up with arguments, disrupted, erratic or unusual schedules, strangers in the house, extreme mood swings from your parents, or your family may experience financial problems.
- It's not okay for you to be put in this position and no-one should make you feel that your parents' behaviour is your fault. It is not your fault.

- The best place to start is to call Kids Helpline on 1800 55 1800 or visit their website www.kidshelp.com.au and get some advice about your situation and what you can do.
- You may feel guilty about contacting a service for advice and support—but it is the right thing to do. Your health and wellbeing, and the wellbeing of your brothers and sisters, is the most important thing in this situation.
- If your safety and wellbeing is ever threatened—please call emergency services on '000' straightaway.

Charlotte Beaumont-Field

Wellbeing Manager, Inspire Foundation

In profile: Tom

Age: 30

Hair colour: Brown

Eye colour: Brown

Favourite saying: 'There's always more.'

Greatest personal moment: I consider every moment that I become aware of the synchronicity in my life to be the greatest moments.

Dream yet to accomplish: Wow . . . there are so many. Climbing Everest is definitely one of them . . . and I've booked a trip to Everest for next May.

Favourite colour: It's a toss-up between blue and green.

Favourite place in the world: Italy, it's the most inspiring place and I have the best ideas come to me there. My second favourite place is the shower, for the same reasons as above.

Best tip: Be in the moment.

Favourite quote: Know yourself, trust yourself and remember that the harder you work, the luckier you get.

Dream for my future: That every day, my perception of what I am capable of will grow, and that my perspective of everything in the world will continue to expand.

Worst moment

In Year 4 someone sent a birthday invite to every single person in the class except me.

Medication

At one stage I saw a psychiatrist and his answer was to put me on antidepressants. This lasted for about three weeks. I felt that my issues were emotional and that's what needed to be addressed. So I got off them pretty quickly, and my mum supported me in that decision.

I've done research subsequent to that experience. While everything has a physical manifestation, that doesn't mean that's where it begins. Other issues are at the core.

Response ability

Based on my experiences I have come to this conclusion:

Responsibility = Response Ability.

This means the ability to respond and take total ownership of that response, regardless of the outcome.

Personal insight

During childhood ideals are formed like a glass—a glass that holds your life—and it doesn't matter what you pour into the glass later because that glass is already formed. And as you get older you mould certain experiences to fit in with that first emotionally intense experience. Everything becomes an interpretation seen through the filters of what is in the glass.

POWER STATEMENT

Sharing experiences is one of the most valuable things a person can do. When you share with people, it gives them the opportunity to decide what resonates with them, what they decide to take on and the action that comes as a result of that.

Have you heard of . . .
Youth Insearch
'Love in Action'
www.youthinsearch.org.au

Founded in 1985 by Founding Director Ron Barr AM, the Youth Insearch program provides a safe and trusting environment where young people are encouraged to talk about and share their issues with their peers. This unique approach motivates young people to address the underlying reasons why they turn to negative means of coping, with behavioural issues such as bullying, feeling suicidal, isolation, substance abuse, violence and crime.

Youth Insearch provides the opportunity to go away on weekend programs with other young people suffering from similar issues. Activities designed to empower young people to look inside themselves and reach out to each other create a connectedness and understanding.

They are motivated to seek positive alternatives to current behaviours which are reinforced and encouraged in their own peer support network. This is achieved by weekly support groups, to ensure each young person is able to embark on a program of change while remaining in their own home and school environment.

The model 'peers supporting peers', coupled with a warm and open environment, is the essence of Youth Insearch. All the program youth leaders have come through the Youth Insearch program and therefore have a deep understanding of what it feels like to experience hardship, and the challenges the new participants are experiencing.

Ron and Judith Barr have successfully helped more than 30 000 young people and the demand for the program continues to grow.

'Youth Insearch's "Love in Action" is about people caring for each other without judgement,' Ron says. 'The world presents such confusion and young people have to work through that. The program is the beginning of the healing process. Youth Insearch is about young people helping other young people share their past and believe that they can dare to dream.'

Judith says, 'The young people talk about a feeling of acceptance when they come to the program. It doesn't matter what they've done or where they've come from. That's irrelevant. Youth Insearch is neutral territory.'

What do you do first and foremost to help young people?

Listen without showing any disbelief or shock. Accept the honour that they have chosen to talk with you, let them know they are not alone, that others have had experiences like them and it is important to be able to accept help that will assist them. Either organise to help yourself or organise for someone with the professional expertise to help.

How can a young person best persuade a troubled friend to attend a Youth Insearch program?

By talking about their own experience or a friend's experience. Young people like to know that others have been and experienced the program and that they have had similar experiences.

What is your personal message to young people facing hardship?

You are definitely not alone, nothing is so terrible that there is not a way forward. At a weekend program we would give positive examples of people in the room who have used their disadvantage to their advantage and how they did it.

'After every long dark cold night the sun does shine again.'

In profile: Daniel

Age: 14

Hair colour: Brown

Eye colour: Blue

Dream yet to accomplish: To have a family of my own

Favourite colour: Green

Favourite place in the world: My girlfriend's place because it's peaceful

Best tip: You only get one shot in life so do the best you can.

Favourite quote: 'What goes around comes around.'

Dream for my future: To finish my apprenticeship and join the army

POWER STATEMENT

Forgive yourself. Think of mistakes as an opportunity to learn more about who you are, and change what is no longer working.

Chapter 6

LET'S TALK ABOUT SUICIDE

> 👓 Did you know . . .
>
> Suicide remains one of the leading causes of death among young people aged 15–24, alongside road and traffic accidents.[4]

There is no darker place than when you find yourself all alone, consumed by sadness and despair, and taking your own life seems like the only way to find peace. Death can seem like the ultimate way to escape pain and anguish. You even convince yourself that everyone would be better off if you weren't around. It is hard to believe anything else when you're trapped in the darkness.

Once you take your own life, it's permanent.

If you just hang on, even if it's by a thread, remind yourself that things can't possibly get any worse. This is rock bottom.

There is always a way through. Keep going, believe that you deserve better and things *will* get better.

Open your heart

It's important not to isolate yourself during times of despair. Talk to someone you trust and ask for help. Asking for help may seem like the scariest thing to do, but the people who love you will want to help you. Once you open up, it can feel like a huge burden has been lifted. These are the moments to look inside yourself and find the voice that speaks from your heart; the source of self-love. You are stronger than you know. Listen to what your heart tells you and believe there is a better life waiting for you. Believe that you can change and that one day, you can use this experience to help someone else.

Melinda

'It is one of the most beautiful compensations in life . . . that no man can sincerely try to help another without helping himself.'
Ralph Waldo Emerson

I WAS ON SUICIDE WATCH

I became so helpless and hopeless that I thought seriously about ending my life. I talked to my counsellor about how I intended to do it. I told her that I was at my lowest point and didn't want to live anymore. My counsellor rang my mother, and Mum took me to the hospital emergency ward, where I had to stay on suicide watch. I was confined to a bed, not permitted to move, and I felt terrified and like my personal space had been invaded. It was very lonely and hard to come to terms with.

Lauren

I FANTASISED ABOUT WAYS TO END MY LIFE

As my depression worsened, my thoughts turned suicidal and I fantasised about ending my life and the peace that would follow. I thought if I could just die, there would be nothing to worry about, and nothing would ever bother me again.

But then I thought about how my family would feel if I wasn't around. I knew they'd be devastated, especially my mum. Imagining them in the aftermath of my suicide stopped me from going through with it. At that stage, I was desperate for help and somehow found the courage to confide in my mum.

Mum was amazing. Immediately, she organised for me to see a psychologist and gave me loads of love and support. I firmly believe that if Mum wasn't there to listen and understand, and make me feel worthy of love, that I wouldn't be here today.

Although I love my dad and he wanted to help, he didn't understand what I was going through. I don't feel as though I can talk to him because we don't have an emotional connection, and this hurt me at first. But then I realised that's who Dad is and he's not going to change, and I needed to accept that.

I have two younger sisters and they didn't understand either, and kept their distance from me. At times I felt like an outcast in the family environment. Mum was my rock.

Abby

I once said to someone that I wanted to kill myself. People didn't know how to react and said things like 'No you don't' or 'Don't do that'. They assumed I was mucking around. The fact that they didn't take me seriously made me feel even more alone and invisible.

Abby

Suicide watch—Warning signs

Here are some things to look out for:

- jokes or sarcasm about committing suicide
- sleeping all the time and feeling constantly lethargic
- not doing or enjoying the things they usually like to do
- withdrawing from people and activity.

If you are feeling suicidal

Talk to a trusted adult who can help you find help. Remember:

- There are so many things to look forward to.
- Someone does care about you; you are worth something to someone.
- Someone needs you and loves you and would be devastated if you weren't around.

When my mum said I was her first baby and she was so happy I was born, that made me feel so special. I love my mum and she has helped me so much. I can talk to her about anything and she always listens to me—and *hears* me. My mum is my hero.

Abby

MY FRIENDS TALKED ME OUT OF IT

Two months after my dad and godsister died, I decided I wanted to take my own life. I planned to do it on my birthday. When I started asking my friends 'innocent' questions about taking an overdose of pills, they twigged and confronted me about it. I burst into tears. They convinced me not to do it. I didn't really want to die. It's just that living was so painful.

Natashia

IT MEANS EVERYTHING TO HAVE HOPE

I remember when I was suicidal how much 'better' I felt during and after cutting; the emotional pain trapped inside would gush out of my veins with all the blood. The thought of dying increased every day and I became more 'excited' about it. The only thing holding me back from going through with it was the thread of hope I still held for my future—the family I would selfishly leave behind; the person I wanted to become, the things I wanted to do, the places I wanted to go and, above all, the best, loving, caring and wonderful mother I knew I would be to my oodles of children and a loving and adoring wife to my future husband. These glimmers of hope kept me going through my dark days. Without them I had nothing that I believed was worth living for.

Channel your feelings into something positive

There are other more creative outlets to relieve your anger or depression; simply create or continue a hobby or activity that keeps you calm, happy and changes your mindset from suicide to peace. If you're stuck for ideas, the following might help: writing, listening or singing to music, going for walks or jogs, creative writing, dancing, any drama-related activities, expression through art, taking a younger sibling or beloved pet for a walk or playing with them, and above all talking to somebody that you trust—they may be able to help you.

Alyssa-Kate

An expert's view

Q: MY FRIEND HAS STARTED TALKING ABOUT WAYS SHE PLANS TO TAKE HER LIFE. WHAT SHOULD I DO?

A:

- Tell someone you trust like a teacher, counsellor or relative about what your friend has told you. Your friend may have made you promise not to tell anyone about what they have told you—but this is not a secret that you can keep.
- Listen to your friend and let them know that you are there for them. This may be as simple as sending them messages on a regular basis. Making them feel like they are not alone (even if you don't have all the answers) is very important.

- Take care of yourself—when your friend is going through something like this, it is very upsetting and it's easy to forget to look after your own needs, but it's very important to take some time out for yourself and do things that make you feel good.

Charlotte Beaumont-Field

Wellbeing Manager, Inspire Foundation

Q: WHAT SHOULD I DO IF MY THOUGHTS BECOME SUICIDAL?

A:

- First of all, take it very seriously, your life is at risk.
- Secondly, no matter how much you feel driven to do so, do not cut off or isolate yourself, as it is much harder to get through this alone.
- Thirdly, ask for help, it is the first courageous step to recovery. Tell someone and keep telling someone until you are taken seriously and offered the support you need. Parents will usually be a great support but if not, then try a teacher, friend, school counsellor, someone in your church, a coach or trusted relative or speak to a professional.
- Don't give up. Remember that others may see options that you cannot currently see. Recognise that while it may seem hopeless right now, with help many people recover from depression and/or feeling suicidal and go on to live happy and fulfilled lives.

Tessa Marshall

Director, Marshall Coaching Group

- If you are worried about your thoughts, talk to someone. A good first step can be the school or uni counsellor or your GP. You may need to ask for help more than once before you get the help you need—keep letting different people know until someone listens.
- If you feel people aren't listening to you or giving you what you need, don't be disheartened. There are several steps involved in seeking help and getting to the right person.
- There is a difference between thoughts and actions. There is also a big difference between thinking about death and taking your own life. Ask yourself if you are worried you might do something to yourself—if you are, you need to seek help right away. Treatment for depression and related issues is effective and you can recover.
- If you are unsure, talk to someone who knows you, and who you trust, about what you are thinking and why you think you feel this way.

Vikki Ryall

Clinical Manager, headspace National Office

- It's very important that you tell someone you trust about these thoughts—even if you feel silly or feel that you don't want to stress people out.
- Talk to a counsellor (via web, phone, face to face) about the thoughts you are having. The thoughts you are having can be worked through with the right support and connections.
- Get as much support around you as possible—don't go through it alone.

- Keep yourself safe—work through a safety plan with a counsellor or someone you trust about the things you can do if you are experiencing suicidal thoughts. This plan may include calling a friend/counsellor/helpline, reading inspirational stories, watching an uplifting DVD, writing poems/songs/stories.
- If you are in immediate danger of taking your life, you need to call emergency services on '000' straightaway.

Charlotte Beaumont-Field

Wellbeing Manager, Inspire Foundation

In profile: Lauren

Age: 18

Hair colour: My hair colour changes quite frequently, at the moment it's red-brown.

Eye colour: Blue-grey

Favourite saying: 'Pain is temporary, pride is forever.'

Greatest personal moment: When I got into uni, it was a great achievement as it meant, even with everything I was facing, I still aspired to be and do what I wanted to, and I achieved my goal that was always in the back of my mind.

Dream yet to accomplish: Inspire other young people, and show them there is life after pain and torment; graduate from my course at uni.

Favourite colour: Purple

Favourite place in the world: The beach, it's relaxing and the waves symbolise bringing in the new and washing away the old, a metaphor I like to remember about life. It's where I like to go when I have time to myself.

Best tip: You get out of life what you put in and if you put your mind to it, you can achieve anything you want.

Favourite quote: It takes less energy to forgive and forget than to hold on to the pain someone has caused you.

Dream for my future: Get a job helping young people in danger or who are struggling with certain things in life; travel around Europe and work over there for a while; have a close supportive partner and family; finish writing my book and get it published; be happy and enjoy life

Worst moments

- Feelings of worthlessness and allowing people to treat me badly—I didn't care about or respect myself enough, which in turn affected most of my relationships.
- When Mum went through my room and took away all the sharp objects and emptied my supply of Panadol—I wasn't allowed in my room alone or at home by myself. I had to be around people all the time because everyone was worried I'd commit suicide. All my control mechanisms had been taken away and I was constantly watched. It was a desperately lonely and confusing time when I fought to make sense of my emotions and my place in the world.

POWER STATEMENT

You can get through anything. Struggles make you stronger and they make you who you are. There are always going to be bumps in the road, but the strength you have within you will always be there.

Chapter 7

STRUGGLING WITH EATING ISSUES

👓 Did you know . . .

Just over a third of teens have experienced bullying about their body image—either personally or through their friends' experiences. They believe it is a main contributor to their insecurities.[5]

If you struggle with feelings of hopelessness and feel bad about the way you look, one unkind comment can be enough to push you over the edge and into a pattern of disordered eating. This is a dangerous place because it can lead to extreme dieting and an obsession with food and weight, which can spiral into an eating disorder. Once this self-destructive mindset takes hold, it can be painfully difficult to break the cycle. To suffer from an eating disorder is to live a lonely, miserable existence, where your feelings are dictated by what you put in your mouth and your thoughts focus mainly on food, calories and weight.

As someone who suffered from anorexia, I know only too well the anguish that is all consuming, every moment of every day. Anorexia snatched my dreams, destroyed my relationships and ruined my future. As an advocate for promoting positive body image, I have spoken with many people who have suffered from anorexia, bulimia, binge-eating disorder, exercise bulimia, bigorexia and male anorexia. And I have discovered one common denominator—Every one of these people thought their eating disorder would bring them fulfilment and happiness. In fact, the opposite was true. And the hardest part is finding the strength and the will to break free.

If you have an eating disorder, I promise that recovery is possible. Support from experts and the people who love you can help you find your path to recovery. You are far from alone. Recovery takes persistence and determination, but it is absolutely possible. Life on the other side is amazing; when I recovered I finally knew what it felt like to live with freedom and peace.

Melinda

BEING BULLIED LED TO ANOREXIA AND BULIMIA

I developed anorexia when I was sixteen and over time this turned into bulimia. I've had issues with weight most of my life. When I was young, my father pushed me against a wall and called me a 'stupid fat cow'. At school I was bullied about my weight. I have never been able to forget these things, and attribute my struggle with weight and self-esteem to these incidents, as well as an episode of sexual abuse when I was ten.

My father makes remarks about my weight, even in front of my boyfriend. Because my father constantly puts me down I really struggle with my body image and I'm still learning to be truly happy with myself.

Lauren

Parents have so much power over their children and can take away their self-esteem with one sentence.
Lauren

DAD MADE ME FEEL WORTHLESS

When I scored 98 per cent in a maths exam, I was elated. I told my father and his response was 'What happened to the other 2 per cent?' Instead of celebrating my success, he made a point about the fact that I didn't do better. This was a pattern with him. It didn't matter how well I thought I did, he always wanted to know why I didn't do better. I ended up developing an eating disorder because I felt so worthless. I started to wonder why people liked me. It took a lot of work with a therapist to undo the belief that I wasn't good enough and to love and accept myself as I am without the need for approval from others.

Ally

I COULDN'T STOP EATING

Being the only chubby girl in my group really upset me, and no matter how many compliments I was given, it didn't make a difference. I cried privately in the change rooms when clothes didn't fit. And at times during conflict I would be called a 'fat bitch', which tipped me over the edge. Food was my escape; I had no control, I would just eat, eat and eat.

Veronica

MY STEPMOTHER TRIED TO STARVE ME TO DEATH

Living with my stepmum became a game of survival. There were six children and we were all 'ranked' from most to least important. Her children came first, followed by my sister and then me. Due to the starvation we would fight each other for crumbs of food.

I became 'forcibly anorexic'. My father and stepmother neglected my health and my stepmother tried to starve me to death. It got to the point where her own family secretly gave me money to spend at the school canteen and corner store on the way home from school. I also resorted to stealing money—anything I found at home that I could buy food with was mine. As wrong as it was (and I understood this) desperate times called for desperate measures. My sister couldn't do anything to help me even if she tried. It was a dog-eat-dog-world at home and she had to look out for herself.

By age twelve I was severely underweight and was put on suicide watch where teachers and my counsellor looked out for me, until I was about fifteen. I was never properly treated for anorexia because my father feared the public health system. He knew they would ask questions and would need answers—and he would lose us if they knew the truth.

Alyssa-Kate

I would get up in the mornings (if I had the strength) and look in the mirror in disbelief at the sickening and ghastly skeleton staring back at me and say, 'How I wish I could die today, not because I REALLY want to but because living like this I'd rather die a quick and painless death, than slowly rot.'

Alyssa-Kate

Strategies to recover

When I decided that anorexia was no longer an option, this is what helped me the most:

- finding a therapist or counsellor I felt comfortable opening up to
- getting angry at the eating disorder for everything it took from me
- becoming conscious of my thoughts so I could start to identify triggers; trying to let go of negative thought processes and shift into a more positive mindset

- writing down my reasons for wanting to let go of the eating disorder and referring to them often
- focusing on achieving physical as well as emotional wellness
- reminding myself that I am a wonderful person who deserves to be happy
- keeping a list of things that I loved to do, like walking in the sunshine or watching a comedy flick, and doing one of these things if I felt sad or down.

Melinda

An expert's view

Eating disorders comprise a range of mental health problems where sufferers become pre-occupied with their weight, body shape and appearance, and take radical and unhealthy measures to control their weight—such as extreme dieting and fasting, vomiting, abuse of laxatives, diuretics and other substances, and excessive exercising.

The stereotype of a person with an eating disorder is a female in her late teens or twenties. However, eating disorders can start as early as seven or eight, and be found in people in their 70s and 80s. One in ten adult sufferers is male. Males sometimes develop conditions informally called 'manorexia', where extreme weight control and body image issues are accompanied by a preoccupation with attaining a buffed muscular body.

Eating disorders can be a way of coping with difficulties or dealing with emotions like anger or depression. Sufferers can end up defining their self-worth through their appearance and weight, and their life can be taken over by the mental preoccupation and activities associated around food, weight loss and hiding their problems. Most worryingly, serious illness and even death can result from an eating disorder.

On the positive side, eating disorders can be cured, and the sooner they are identified, the better. Early warning signs include:

- eating alone or avoiding social functions because eating is involved
- dropping off from previous social and leisure interests
- rapid weight loss or weight gain
- other people saying you look slim, where you feel you look fat.

Seeking help

This can be the most difficult and yet most important step. It can be terrifying for some people to acknowledge they have a problem and take the 'risk' to give up the behaviours and beliefs of an eating disorder that feel essential to survival. Motivation to change is the key ingredient, and sometimes it can be helpful weighing up the pros and cons of changing before making the decision to change.

An obstacle to seeking help is often a sense of shame or guilt for 'doing this to myself'. However, there is some evidence that there is a genetic component to eating disorders. Some people may be more prone to these difficulties than others.

Friends and families can make a huge difference to someone suffering from an eating disorder. Giving messages of care and understanding, resisting tendencies to pressure or criticise, standing by, and gently nudging them towards recognising that they have a problem that they may wish to seek help for can be the best thing you can do.

Further information about eating disorders can be found at www.cedd.org.au or email info@cedd.org.au.

Jeremy Freeman
Centre for Eating & Dieting Disorders (CEDD),
Sydney, Australia

Have you heard of . . .
The Butterfly Foundation
www.thebutterflyfoundation.org.au

The Butterfly Foundation is dedicated to changing culture, policies and practices in the prevention and treatment of eating disorders. We provide support for those who suffer from eating disorders and negative body image issues and for those who love them.

Eating disorders are serious, life-threatening mental illnesses. They are not a lifestyle choice. They are predominantly about feelings, not food.

We promote positive body image and encourage hope and the seeking of help through education and awareness.

The Butterfly Foundation believes that the respect, compassion and understanding that sufferers of eating disorders deserve will only be achieved through awareness and education campaigns and programs in schools, the health service sector and the wider community.

What should you do if you think you have an eating issue?

If you are worried that feelings you have about food and your body are stopping you from enjoying your life, friends, family and hobbies, the following tips may help:

- Find a trusted person to talk to, such as a teacher, your mum or dad, or a friend. Let them know how you are feeling as openly as you can. Talking about your problem can give you some breathing space and help lift a weight from your shoulders. It also gives someone who cares for you an opportunity to help.
- If you are very worried about yourself or know that there is a serious problem you need addressed— make an appointment to visit your doctor as soon as you can. They can help you by giving you a full medical check-up and providing you with referrals to professionals who can help further, such as a counsellor or psychologist.

Speak up! It's not okay for anyone to feel unhappy about the way they look, including you!

How can you best start to work towards recovery?

Recovery from an eating disorder does not happen overnight, it is something that takes acceptance and hard work over a period of time. The length and pathway towards recovery and freedom from an eating disorder is different for everyone, but it is important to remember that 100 per cent recovery is always possible. There is always hope.

Here are some tips to assist you on getting to the right path:

- Ask for help from friends and family. An eating disorder mindset can be isolating and debilitating, so getting support and understanding from people around you can be helpful in having feedback about the negative thoughts you may be having.
- Establish support. No matter how long you have been experiencing disordered eating, it is important to consult your doctor for an assessment and ongoing check-ups. Your doctor will be able to monitor your physical and psychological health and link you to the right supports.
- Perseverance and patience—an eating disorder does not develop overnight, it is a complex illness which

develops over time. As a result, overcoming the eating disorder mindset takes patience and perseverance, as you work with your supports on undoing the distorted messages and beliefs ingrained in you by the illness.

What should you do if you suspect your friend is suffering from an eating disorder?

When you are worried that someone you care about might have an eating disorder, it can be hard knowing the right way to talk to them about your concerns. In thinking about an approach to take, it might be helpful for you to remember that the best way to assist someone you have concerns for is to address the problem as early as possible, in a caring, empathetic and supportive way. Please remember that an eating disorder will not disappear if it is ignored.

- Consider and plan the best words, time and place to raise your concerns with your friend. More than likely your friend will be more receptive if you engage them in a calm conversation using non-blaming language to highlight your concerns for them.
- Find an adult you feel comfortable with to talk about how you are feeling and what is happening with your friend.
- Inform yourself about eating disorders. By arming yourself with information, you can provide your friend with support and treatment options.

- Be prepared for a strong emotional response from your friend. They may feel scared or threatened that you have discovered the eating disorder, but this doesn't mean they don't want or appreciate your concern. It is important for you to remember that what they are experiencing can be extremely challenging and difficult and they may require some time to absorb your message.

- Focus on feelings and your observations in a non-blaming way, rather than making comments about your friend's weight, eating behaviours or appearance. By focusing on your observations about the concerning things you have noticed, as well as how this makes you feel, your friend may be able to build an understanding of how the illness is beginning to negatively affect their life and their relationships with others.

- Reassure your friend that you are there for them and will stick by them while they get help and recover.

In profile: Abby

Age: 16

Hair colour: Black

Eye colour: Brown

Favourite saying: 'Oh my God.'

Dream yet to accomplish: To be a beauty therapist in my own beautiful shop

Favourite colour: Pink

Favourite place in the world: My bedroom because it's where I get to sleep

Best tip: Live life the way you want, not how others want you to. Do things that make you happy.

Favourite quote: 'What goes around comes around.'

Dream for my future: To be married and have children, living a happy life

On thin ice

At school I was painfully shy. People used to say I gave them filthy looks but the truth was I'd be lost in my own world, depressed and upset, and people took it the wrong way.

When I'd walk to school, I would feel a nervous sickness in the pit of my stomach. My skin prickled with perspiration, my heart started beating faster and I'd feel hot and flustered, consumed with worry about running late. When I arrived I felt as though everyone was looking at me, talking behind my back. I never raised my hand in class because I was worried about what other people would say or think, and I'd stay away from certain areas where I knew my peer group hung out, because they could be cruel and judgemental. I would have given anything not to worry about what other people thought of me.

Toughest moment

I was having a terrible day and my sister and I got into a horrible fight. She said cruel things about my weight. The taunts became too much and I retreated to my room and swallowed a handful of tablets in an attempt to overdose. It didn't work and I felt even more worthless.

POWER STATEMENT

Live your life the way *you* want to live it and do the things that make *you* happy, not other people.

Chapter 8

STARING INTO THE DEPTHS OF DEPRESSION

Did you know . . .

Adolescent depression is one of the most frequently reported mental health problems. More than a quarter of Australians aged 18–24 are currently living with an anxiety or substance abuse disorder.[6]

I want to tell you that everything's going to be alright—but when you're suffering from depression that can be the hardest thing to believe. Dark thoughts and feelings can warp your judgement and skew situations so they seem much worse than they are. For a while (before and during anorexia) dark feelings lurched up and grabbed hold of me, suffocating me with their toxicity. If someone had told me there was a way back from the darkness, I don't know if I would have believed them.

But there was a way back, and I found it.

You can make it through

I am here to let you know, with absolute certainty, that there *is* a way back from the darkness. Your journey will be different to mine but, ultimately, you can conquer this. You can turn those feelings around and use them to motivate you and make your life better.

Melinda

I FELT SUFFOCATED BY EXHAUSTION

I was diagnosed with depression when I was fifteen and given antidepressants. I'd start crying for no reason, I would rather curl up in bed and stay there than face each day. Mum had to come in each morning and drag me out of bed or I didn't get up. I didn't know why I was so sad, or why I couldn't eat or sleep but was always tired. I couldn't understand it. It felt as though everything was getting on top of me and I had no control over what emotions I felt and how I reacted.

Lauren

I COULDN'T DEAL WITH DAD'S DEATH

When I was eight my mother's boyfriend moved in with us. I got along with him well, mostly because he made my mum happy. But he wasn't my dad.

When I was thirteen my liver failed and I was diagnosed with hemochromatosis, where you absorb too much iron from an ordinary diet, and then depression. Depression is hereditary in my family, but I also feel this was brought on by the death of my father, and my inability to express my grief and guilt.

I felt helpless and hopeless and although I was seeing a counsellor, I didn't really like to talk about my feelings. I think this was my way of staying numb, of not having to deal with the incredible pain I kept trying to push away.

Then my brother attended a youth camp and raved about it. He tried to convince me to join him. He went to six of these camps, and his last was my first—he dragged me kicking and screaming.

The camp was one of the best things I've ever done. Everyone there listened to me without judgement, and made me feel loved and welcome. I had the best time and didn't want to go home.

Jasmin

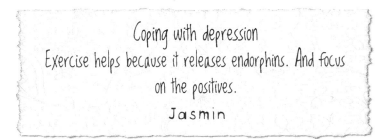

Coping with depression
Exercise helps because it releases endorphins. And focus on the positives.
Jasmin

More information
The MoodGYM: www.moodgym.anu.edu.au/
YBBLUE—youth depression website: www.beyondblue.org.au/ybblue/
Beyond Blue: www.beyondblue.org.au
Mensline (Youth Services): www.menslineaus.org.au/Youth/

An expert's view

While there are still many questions yet to be answered by research into depression and anxiety, stress is definitely a contributing factor. Genes, physical and chemical factors and general lifestyle can trigger depression and anxiety, but stress is also very frequently a key cause.

Stress itself, however, can be a positive factor in your life. 'Good' stress motivates you, gives you drive and heightens your alertness and thought clarity. It only becomes 'bad' stress when it stops you from functioning healthily. This occurs if the situation causing the stress cannot be easily resolved. Examples are living in situations of domestic violence, child abuse, neglect, bullying, poverty, or trauma, loss of a loved one and other losses such as friendships, future dreams or physical injury. Study pressures and pressures to conform or feel included as part of a group can also lead to ongoing stress.

The best cure is to avoid becoming overloaded. Look after your wellbeing: exercise regularly, maintain a healthy diet, make time for things that you enjoy each and every day, manage your time to achieve things that must be done, take time out from stress-inducing situations whenever you can, and get enough sleep.

Tessa Marshall
Director, Marshall Coaching Group

In profile: Veronica

Age: 18

Hair colour: Brown with a blonde strip on left-hand side

Eye colour: Brown

Favourite saying: 'You never know how strong you are until being strong is the only choice you have.'

Greatest personal moment: Singing to an audience

Dream yet to accomplish: Have a family and travel the world

Favourite colour: Red

Favourite place in the world: The beach, because I wash my worries away

Best tip: When life bites you, bite it back harder.

Favourite quote: 'I don't have a weight problem, people just gotta problem with my weight.' *Phat Girlz*

Dream for my future: To be the best I can, to be as happy as I can and to be a great mother to my children and a happy wife to my husband

POWER STATEMENT
Being strong was the only choice I had.

Q: WHAT SHOULD I DO IF I'M DEPRESSED OR HAVE SELF DESTRUCTIVE THOUGHTS?

A: Self-destructive thoughts can be very powerful and dangerous. They can pull you into a downward spiral very quickly unless you are aware your thoughts have become dark and negative, know your triggers and symptoms, and have ways of responding when they occur. (See p. 160 for more about triggers.) Having some coping mechanisms in your tool-kit is an essential part of breaking the spiral. You may want to:

- Speak to your doctor as medication can sometimes help and it is worth ruling out any physical triggers.
- Slow down your breathing if you notice it becoming rapid.
- Take time out to regroup if you find yourself in a situation that is a trigger for you.
- Speak assertively and make a request for change if another person's behaviour is impacting on you.
- Seek help from a friend.
- Do things you love doing, things that promote self-nurture.
- Ask yourself, 'What would I advise a friend to do if they were going through what I'm going through?'
- Help others in some way. There is much evidence to support helping others as a way of feeling more worthwhile yourself and giving you perspective on the issues you have.
- Write a note like 'Breathe, it will get better', put it somewhere you will read it every day and then read it out to yourself and slow your breathing each and every hour.

Tessa Marshall
Director, Marshall Coaching Group

Looking after yourself will support your mental health. Try to keep regular sleeping, eating and exercise habits. Try to stick to your routine (work, study, hobbies, etc.) as much as possible, even if it feels like the last thing you want to do. If you look after yourself by allowing your body adequate rest and nourishment, and stick to a routine that works for you, this can have an extremely positive impact on your mental health.

Look at the relationship between feelings, thoughts and behaviour. When we feel down or sad, we are more likely to interpret the world negatively or have negative thoughts. Noticing the relationship between your thoughts, feelings and actions can help you make changes in these things. When you start to feel bad or have negative thoughts that unsettle you and you find hard to get rid of, try to talk about how you are feeling with someone you trust.

We can learn a lot about ourselves and our needs in relationships with others. It is within relationships (family, friends, etc.) that we learn to express ourselves, communicate our needs and, importantly, how to cope if our needs can't be met. If you don't feel okay and feel like you need some support, let someone you trust know. If you ask for what you need you are more likely to get it; people can't read your mind.

Vikki Ryall

Clinical Manager, headspace National Office

Chapter 9

DRUGS—A MASK FOR HEARTACHE

It feels as though the world is ending. You don't care about anything anymore. Life sucks and no-one seems to understand or even care how helpless and hopeless you're feeling.

Then someone offers you drugs. So you take them, get high and love the feeling of being invincible, as though nothing can touch you. Then you come crashing down when it all wears off and life seems bleak and hollow once more. You crave that feeling of being high, where there is no pain, only a sense of control. If only you could feel that way in everyday life. Sound familiar?

Finding the way back

When bad stuff happens drugs can seem like an easy solution to make it all go away. But there can be devastating consequences, including a change in personality, losing friends, even going to gaol.

If a friend pulls you aside and tells you they are concerned about your behaviour, it is coming from somewhere so hear them out. And if you know somewhere deep within yourself that taking drugs is wrong but you don't know how to stop, don't be afraid to ask for help. You are stronger than you know and there are so many people who will want to be there and give you the support you need. It doesn't mean you're a bad person. We all derail from time to time. There are some contacts at the end of this chapter that you may find useful.

Finding the way back can be difficult and painful but there *is* a way back. The first step is putting up your hand and asking for help.

Melinda

I WAS HOOKED ON ECSTASY

While I was sixteen my issues really began. I became dangerously overconfident, I wasn't afraid to get hurt and I didn't care. I just thought I could do whatever I wanted, whenever. I would work during the week and on weekends I'd pop ecstasy. I'd drink, smoke and dance. I got into a few fights; one of my girlfriends had a gun put to her head while we were celebrating a friend's birthday at a local park, and I almost got stabbed a few months later at a restaurant because I yelled at a guy who was threatening my friend. I got into a street fight. It was just a horrible life. I wasn't going in the right direction and the hole in my heart was getting bigger.

My mother realised how serious my issues were getting. I would call her and say, 'Mum I'm not coming home'. She would argue with me but I didn't care—I stayed out anyway. I was caught smoking pot at school on my sixteenth birthday and was suspended for three days.

Veronica

STEALING BECAME THE ONLY WAY TO FEED MY HABIT

My friend's dad tried to rape me once and I pressed charges. After this, I ran away a lot. I usually stayed at friends' houses but sometimes me and my friends would break into abandoned houses and sleep there. I was drinking and doing drugs every weekend. I was getting into fights with people I didn't like or sometimes even strangers that looked at me the wrong way. I stole from people at school; I usually stole money but sometimes I would steal other things like phones and iPods because my friends wanted them. Eventually I got caught and was suspended for ten days.

After I was suspended I ran away and was eventually picked up by the police. I was taken home and my mum told me to pack my bags and that she was taking me to live with my aunty. I liked my aunty, although I didn't know her as well as my other family members, who did not like her. But the worst part was I felt like I was being abandoned by my mum.

The worst moment was when I found out that my counsellor had died from cancer. I ran away that night. The next morning I was with my friend and we were winding down from the drugs and alcohol we'd had the night before to forget about it all. We were hungry so we broke into a car and stole some bread. I felt so bad because of what I had to do just to feed myself and because I was sobering up it made me realise how screwed up my behaviour had become. Later that day we were planning on mugging a girl we saw walking past us but she got into a car before we had the chance. We were extremely desperate for food and more drugs and it was really hard at the time. The measures I had to go to just to survive were horrendous. I hated having to resort to mugging someone so I could eat and get high. When the girl we were planning to mug got into the car, in a way I felt relieved that she was safe. She was an innocent person and I suddenly realised that what I was doing was wrong and that she should have the right to walk the streets and feel safe.

Meg

✍

More information
NDARC—Australian website on alcohol and drugs:
www.ndarc.med.unsw.edu.au/
Comprehensive Australian Alcohol and Drug
Information Network: www.adin.com.au
Education Centre Against Violence (ECAV):
www.ecav.health.nsw.gov.au
Father Chris Riley's Youth Off the Streets:
www.youthoffthestreets.com.au

An expert's view

Q: WHAT SHOULD I DO IF MY FRIEND IS TAKING DRUGS AND/OR BEING DESTRUCTIVE?

A: Let your friend know that you are really worried about what they're doing. Seek information about what your friend is involved with and read up on it. Have a look at the headspace website at www.headspace.org.au. Another great resource is the Reach Out website at www.reachout.com.au, where you will find fact sheets on how to help your friend.

Encourage the people in your life to be honest, and practise honesty yourself.

There is nothing wrong with saying, 'I'm worried about what you're doing. I think you need some help and I'm happy to come with you.'

If your friend doesn't feel like they have a problem, keep giving the message that you're concerned by their behaviour. Check with your other friends to see if they're worried as well. If it gets worse, it's okay to say, 'I'm so worried now that I feel I have no other choice but to let an adult/someone else know.' This might anger your friend, but all you can do is be honest. Even if it's seen as uncool, your friend's wellbeing is at stake.

It might also benefit you to talk to someone about getting help to help your friend.

Vikki Ryall
Clinical Manager, headspace National Office

Chapter 10

WHEN DRINKING GETS OUT OF CONTROL

As with drugs, drinking to get drunk can be a mask for pain and heartache. It may also be something you do because all your friends are doing it. When you're in the moment, it can be hard to say no. Drinking slows down thinking and interferes with concentration. Too much drinking alters behaviour. You may wind up doing something you wouldn't normally do and if it's something that can't be undone, you're left to face the consequences.

Take positive action to avoid drinking too much

If you feel guilty about drinking too much, have done something you regret while drinking, or use alcohol to cope with unhappiness, the first step is acknowledging your feelings and thinking about the reasons behind your behaviour. If you are experiencing negative feelings, think about what is making you unhappy. What are some ways that you can take positive action to deal with the situation the best way you can?

How you feel about yourself and the way you treat yourself sets the benchmark for others. Remember that asking for help can be a great way to put things in perspective and tackle stressful situations in a way that is proactive—instead of destructive.

Melinda

MY BEST FRIEND DOBBED ME IN

When I was fifteen one of my friends brought vodka to school. I was feeling really down that day, so I had some. My best friend at the time dragged me to the teacher, who took me to the office to see the deputy principal, and I got suspended for two days. I felt helpless and didn't know what else I could do at the time, which is why I did it. Mum said that it was a mistake and let me off lightly. I think she knew I was going through a rough time, and didn't want to make me feel worse.

Lauren

DAD GAVE ME ALCOHOL

Due to my depression, I overdosed on anything I could get hold of and cut myself just about wherever I could—I still have scars. Lastly I resorted to alcohol (something I was around quite frequently). My father condoned underage drinking.

I was about eleven or twelve when I was given 25 mL of pina colada. I drank the more exotic drinks with higher alcoholic content growing up with my father.

Alyssa-Kate

DRINKING NUMBED THE PAIN

I hated being at home because of Mum and Dad fighting all the time, so I'd leave for days on end and drink alcohol to escape the pain. It made me feel better for a while, until I sobered up. I was out of control but I didn't know how else to handle things.

Justin

I BINGE-DRANK EVERY WEEKEND

After losing Dad and my godsister, I became distant. I started skipping school. My friends turned against me because they didn't understand me anymore. I got in with the wrong crowd and when I begged my brother to throw me a party the weekend my mother was out of town, I invited everyone I could think of. The house was packed. I downed so much alcohol that I was off my face. I didn't know what I was doing, and all my so-called guy friends told me to flash people. I thought I was so cool. Then the police came and broke up the party.

Everyone at school heard about me flashing and all these rumours started. People were whispering about me behind my back, calling me a slut.

All my old friends dumped me.

I stopped studying and went wild. Every weekend I was at a different party, drunk and out of control. I decided to make 'flashing' my trademark. (In hindsight, one of the stupidest things I've ever done.)

One day, when I skipped school, I went to a friend's house and got drunk. I bumped into my ex on the way home and he tried to take advantage of me. I decided, to get away from him, I'd go downtown and continue drinking. Again I started flashing everyone. I was so messed up. I felt as though I had no-one. My mother was never home, and she'd kicked my brothers out.

I became fed up with all the rumours about me that I decided to lose my virginity and get it over with. So I did it with a guy I hardly knew when I was drunk. Everyone heard about it and all the rumours got worse.

I spun even further out of control and did a nude run at another party. I constantly wagged school. I was hanging out with a rough crowd and binge-drinking every weekend.

At the parties, people would arrive with backpacks full of grog. Everywhere guys and girls were hooking up, dirty dancing, having sex. There were girls staggering around blind drunk. Fights breaking out. Lots of underage sex, people having threesomes. Loads of drugs: speed, ecstasy, marijuana.

Promiscuous girls would come to school on Monday bragging about who they'd slept with as though it was cool. But lots of girls at these parties get raped. Some guys are predators, waiting for girls to get drunk. One time a girl got raped at a party and there were people standing around but no-one did anything. It happens so often and people don't want to get involved.

On a school excursion, two girls in my year bought vodka on the trip. One girl drank half the bottle and passed out. All her friends tried to hide her from the teacher. She slipped into a semi-coma, vomiting while unconscious. Her friends became terrified and eventually told the teacher. This girl was given a 70–80 per cent chance of surviving. The bottom line was, if her friends hadn't told at all, she would have died. If they hadn't told when they did, she would have suffered severe brain damage. This girl was on the school representative council. Everyone lost so much respect for her.

Natashia

Alcohol alters your behaviour and binge-drinking is dangerous. Everyone judges you. It's not worth the consequences—the rumours, the loss of respect, not only by your peers, but your self-respect too.
Drinking isn't the answer. When everyone else is drinking and you want to fit in, it is so hard to say no. People tried to push me all the time. Finally I realised, I just had to say no and be definite about it. Remember, if it doesn't feel right, don't do it.

Natashia

EVERYONE'S WASTED

I witnessed kids getting wasted every weekend. Often people in my class would turn up to school with hangovers. People brought alcohol to school. There was a smoker's corner where people would hide away from the teachers and smoke cigarettes. It's so easy to get drugs. Everything is accessible.

I never fell into this side of school life because, as a result of being bullied, I didn't have much confidence so I kept to myself.

Watching other people get wasted all the time and brag about it disturbed me though.

What should you do?

If you sense a friend is troubled and needs help, or is drinking to extreme and is in denial, approach them as a trusted friend and tell them you are worried about them and want to help. Offer to go to counselling with them.

James

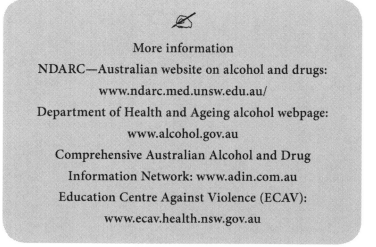

More information
NDARC—Australian website on alcohol and drugs:
www.ndarc.med.unsw.edu.au/
Department of Health and Ageing alcohol webpage:
www.alcohol.gov.au
Comprehensive Australian Alcohol and Drug
Information Network: www.adin.com.au
Education Centre Against Violence (ECAV):
www.ecav.health.nsw.gov.au

An expert's view

WHAT MAKES A DRINKING SESSION A 'BINGE'?

The answer depends on who you listen to. Basically, a 'binge' is an excessive amount of alcohol within a given period. But still—who gets to say what is 'excessive'? You can probably form your own opinion. If you ever considered the day after drinking that there were any downsides to your drinking, then it was excessive. The official advice from health authorities is that women should not exceed two standard drinks[7] per day on average over a week, and never more than four drinks in one day. For men, the recommendations are to not exceed four standard alcoholic drinks per day on average and never more than six per day. So, if you are a woman, and you drink more than four standard drinks, then we can safely call that a binge. Other women know that just two or three is too many for them.

> One standard drink is one 30 mL nip of plain spirits (e.g. vodka), a 285 mL middy of beer or a 120 mL glass of wine. A schooner of beer or a premix can of spirits or 180 mL glass of wine is 1½ standard drinks.

Here is a quick checklist to see if your drinking may be a problem:

- Have you ever felt guilty about your drinking?
- Have you ever hidden how much you have drunk from others?
- Have you ever done something while drinking that you regret or embarrassed you?
- Have you ever 'blacked out' (losing time) due to alcohol?
- Have you ever drunk alcohol to manage negative feelings or cope with situations?
- Have you ever worried about the amount of money you spent on alcohol?
- Have you ever had an accident (e.g. falling over) due to alcohol?
- Have you ever had legal problems (e.g. due to drink driving or violence)?

If you answered 'yes' to any of these questions, then you probably have or have had a problem with alcohol.

If there are so many possible regrets and downsides (like the list above), why do so many of us drink too much at times? The most common reasons include:

- wanting to be part of the majority; fitting in; keeping up with what others are doing
- needing alcohol to manage difficult feelings, like being upset about a relationship, feeling sad or lonely, or to help cope with anxiety in social situations, or needing to relax at the end of the day
- losing track of how much we are drinking and forgetting what a healthy limit is for us.

WHAT CAN YOU DO TO PREVENT BINGE-DRINKING?

Prevention

Prevention is best started by reviewing your own motivation well before you go out or start to drink. Here are some examples of 'motivational questions' that can help you to clear up in your mind what you want to do:

- What do you hate the most about binge-drinking (hangovers, mistakes, angry friends, getting into dangerous situations, cost, etc.)?
- How will you feel in the morning if you've ended up drinking way too much?
- What will people think about you if you lose control?
- How good will you feel about yourself if your night goes really well and you stay in control?

Talk about it

Build up an anti-binge drinking culture among your friends. Start talking regularly about what you think of people who get so intoxicated that they treat themselves or others badly. Talk about how to sometimes drink but keep it under control. Talk about positive ways to have fun without damage to reputation or exposure to risks. The idea is that, with time, you can create a mini-culture for your group of having fun without binge-drinking. If you have some friends who drink heavily and you can't shift that, then plan carefully how you socialise with them.

Plan

The next step is to plan. If you are going out with friends, plan where you will be, how you will get there and get home again. Also, plan how to have fun without having to drink. If you do intend to drink some alcohol, plan how many drinks you can safely have over the whole evening and work out roughly how to space those drinks out.

Know your emotions

Be aware of your emotional state and take some steps to manage your feelings. Some people work out that they are most likely to binge-drink (and do other self-destructive things) in response to certain emotions, like feeling worthless or lonely or worried. If you are in a vulnerable state emotionally, then be very careful about drinking at all, as alcohol can make such feelings worse. Try talking to a friend about how you feel or ask to do something else other than drinking alcohol (like going to the movies or having a night in together).

Pace yourself

Once you have already had one or more drinks, it is very important to count and pace your drinks. Counting involves keeping track of how much you've been drinking. The only reliable way to count your drinks is to know what one 'standard drink' is (see box on p. 121). This is because different alcoholic drinks have different percentages or strengths of alcohol. If someone keeps filling your drink up (like at a party or restaurant), ask them to wait until you have had one at a time. Pacing means sticking to your plan of a certain number of drinks spread out over the evening. It also means having at least one non-alcoholic drink in between every alcoholic one.

MY FRIEND BINGE-DRINKS EVERY WEEKEND AND I'M WORRIED. HOW CAN I PERSUADE HER TO SEEK HELP?

A person usually seeks help when they see:

1. that there is little to lose from getting help
2. that the cost of not seeking help is high
3. where to go and how to access help.

So, if you are worried about someone, then it makes sense to tell them. Try not to be judgemental or label them—like calling them a 'drunk' or 'slut' or 'bad friend'. Rather, point out that some of their behaviours (either their drinking or what they do when drinking) make them less fun to be around and harder to respect. Raise other specific problems that you see and explain why you are worried. Be prepared for repetition—sometimes it takes a few conversations before a person starts to act.

Finally, try to give them some definite options. Try to get a recommendation for a psychologist from someone (like your GP or a parent or school counsellor) so that you can offer them a known health professional or service. Most people that you might ask for that advice would be delighted to help and pleased that something positive is being done to help someone with a problem that is serious but common.

WHAT DOES THE COUNSELLING PROCESS INVOLVE?

The psychologist or counsellor will conduct an assessment of what you would like to change and more generally where you are up to in life. Then you and the counsellor select one or more goals together and work out a good strategy to achieve those goals. Exactly what is the right intervention differs from one person to another and there are many different approaches that are effective. Most interventions include counselling for underlying problems—like managing difficult emotions or coping with family or relationship concerns—and behavioural strategies to help you achieve desired changes in your drinking behaviour pretty soon.

A good counselling process will be friendly and strictly confidential. The psychologist will be keen to identify and help with issues other than drinking too, like social confidence, anxiety, depression and relationships. When we are helped to understand these issues better, we are often more able to drink in a healthier way.

In addition to individual counselling, Alcoholics Anonymous (AA) provides a free community, group-based way for people to work on their drinking. People attend groups that are open to anyone and use these to work through 'steps' towards being completely sober (not drinking any alcohol ever again).

WHAT ARE THE EFFECTS OF DRINKING TOO MUCH ALCOHOL?

To learn about the effects of drinking alcohol, we need to look separately at the immediate effects of any one binge as well as the effects of drinking excessively over months or years. The immediate effects of drinking alcohol include:

- poor decision making
- less inhibitions (we do things we would not normally consider acceptable)
- feeling relaxed and not caring so much
- initial positive feeling, followed by feeling tired
- reduced reaction time
- incoordination.

Longer-term effects of drinking too much repeatedly include:

- damage to liver (increased chance of hepatitis and cirrhosis)
- damage to brain cells (affecting your memory, concentration and judgement)
- weakened muscles
- changes to your blood vessels and heart
- erectile dysfunction in males
- increased likelihood of depression
- increased likelihood of various cancers.

There are some special considerations to take into account if you are young (under 25 years). If you are in this age group, then your brain is still developing and so the damaging effects on brain cells is greater. Also, young people are less likely to be experienced with the effects of alcohol or being able to gauge when to slow down or stop drinking. The smaller you are, the greater the effect of alcohol and the less you can drink; and young women process alcohol very differently from men and their bodies can tolerate much less alcohol. Also, when you are young, it is extra difficult to deal with stressful interactions (like aggression or sexual coercion) at the best of times and alcohol just makes it ten times harder to deal with such situations.

Dr Chris Basten Ph.D.

Clinical psychologist

Have you heard of . . .

Oasis Youth Support Network

www.salvos.org.au/oasis

'Saving Young Lives Daily'

Oasis gives homeless and disadvantaged young people hope, help and opportunities to access relevant education, training, jobs, counselling and drug/alcohol programs. Participants learn work and life skills to help rebuild their lives and develop self-esteem, confidence, community engagement and employability.

Our biggest challenge is creating hope in young people because they feel so hopeless about life. They have picked up messages that tell them they're not valuable and there is no future for them.

Many become involved in harmful activities such as crime, prostitution or drugs, and have suffered physical and emotional abuse. At Oasis, we provide shelter and care, as well as practical solutions with the hope of connecting with these young people.

Our most important task is to inspire hope that these young people can create a better future; a different future, to what they already have.

Some don't see a different path and for those we are constantly trying to create opportunities to help them see there is another path. We provide outdoor adventure and education as well as opportunities and activities that will inspire them, such as music and film. In this way, we attempt to get a spark going so that they start to feel excited and motivated about something.

More often than not, there will come a moment when these young people will want help at a deeper level. This could be a result of a serious legal or health issue, which forces them to realise their situation is not ideal. We need to be there at those moments because they can quickly become a missed opportunity for change.

I believe that actions speak louder than words. Saying to these young people, 'You can do anything you dream of and create an amazing future', can be words that they're not ready to hear or don't believe. Oasis is about creating real opportunities that disconnected young people can actively participate in. We believe everyone can change. No-one is beyond help or beyond hope. These are the principles that guide our work.

Captain Paul Moulds
Director, Oasis Youth Support Network

Chapter 11

WHAT IF YOU THINK YOU'RE GAY?

It can be hard to admit that you're feeling confused about your sexuality. Sometimes it feels safer to keep your feelings to yourself. And then, there are times when being honest about your feelings can help sort through the confusion to figure out who you are and where you're at.

Take your time

If you're feeling confused, it can help to spend some time alone so you have the space to let your emotions drift to the surface. Don't be afraid of what you're feeling. There is no right or wrong. How you feel is how you feel and when you acknowledge your truth, the path will feel less wobbly.

Once you know where you're at, talk to someone you trust so you can figure out the next step and start to gather support.

There are helplines and other resources available so don't feel that you're in this all by yourself. (You'll find some of these at the end of this chapter.) Many people have walked the path before you and while it takes courage to admit that your sexual orientation is same sex or bi-sexual, there are people who are there to listen and understand and who can help you prepare to tell the people you love.

Melinda

COMING OUT WAS THE HARDEST THING I'VE EVER DONE

When I realised I was attracted to women, it was really hard to come to terms with. Like most girls I had my fair share of boyfriends but I always felt that something was missing. I found that I was intrigued by women and developed feelings for one girl in particular who I knew through a mutual friend. I could tell she was interested too, from the looks we exchanged and the way she touched my arm when we talked. The first time we found ourselves alone together, she kissed me and asked if I wanted to see what it was like to be with a woman. I'd never had such intense feelings of desire before and couldn't resist. It felt so different to anything I'd experienced with the boys I'd dated. I felt a passion I'd never known. It felt so right.

Afterwards I struggled with feelings of guilt and shame, but I knew in my heart I was a lesbian. I hid it from everyone for a very long time, until I felt like I was lying to myself by not being truthful about who I was. The process of keeping it a secret was exhausting and I felt increasingly depressed and isolated. I was scared of what people would think of me, and worried my parents might disown me.

I decided to see a counsellor and this was the best thing I could've done because I could openly express myself and my fears to someone unbiased. My counsellor helped me wade through my insecurities and emotions. Once it all came to the surface, it was like a heaviness lifted and I could see myself in a new way. My counsellor helped me realise that I shouldn't ever be ashamed of who I am.

So I decided to find the right time to tell my parents and deal with whatever the consequences.

Carly

I GREW TIRED OF TELLING LIES

The decision to come out was really hard because I was worried what my friends would think, and whether or not they'd accept it. I also knew that gossip about my homosexuality would spread quickly around my school and I could be bullied or harassed.

I'd known for a long time that I was attracted to guys and it wasn't a choice. I had no interest in becoming intimate with a female although I loved female company.

When my mates started losing their virginity and sleeping with girls, I wondered how long it would take before they started to think of me as some kind of weirdo for still being a virgin. I really started to feel the pressure when after weekends, everyone exchanged stories about the people they'd scored with and I was the only one who always seemed to 'luck out'.

It came to a head when my mates set me up with an attractive girl at a party. She led me into one of the bedrooms and tried to seduce me. Part of me wanted to do it just so my friends would back off but I couldn't even kiss her. She ended up in tears asking if I thought she was ugly so I told her I had nausea from nervousness. It was such a pathetic lie but I couldn't tell her the truth. When my mates grilled me about 'the act', I told them she had been a dud so I couldn't go through with it. I felt horrible.

I realised I was spending too much energy telling lies. I'd even lie to my parents about the names of my 'girlfriends'. It became exhausting.

When I told my two closest mates, they were really supportive. One admitted he'd wondered if I was gay, the other said he knew and was waiting for me to be honest about it. I'm not the only gay person at my school and there are a few self-confessed bisexuals as well, so the whole acceptance thing isn't as hard as I thought.

I'm proud of who I am and believe that the more people get to know me well, the less it will be an issue.

Don't expect everyone to be happy for you

The best piece of advice I received from a counsellor at a helpline was this: 'Not everyone will feel happy for you so only tell someone if you think you will be able to handle their reaction and you have enough support around you.' And 'some people believe it is a choice, or that with enough therapy you'll be "cured".'

The reality is I'm still the same person—only now I can live an honest life and not feel as though I have to hide anything.

My parents' reaction

When I told my parents, Mum cried then hugged me and said all she wanted was for me to be happy. Dad shook my hand and patted me on the shoulder, but I could tell from the way his eyes wouldn't meet mine that he was trying to be brave, probably for Mum's sake.

My parents don't talk about it much. I guess they are still coming to terms with the fact that their only son is gay. I hope they will grow to be proud of me for who I am. One day I'd like to bring my future partner to family celebrations.

Jake

BEFORE YOU TELL SOMEONE . . .

Spend some time thinking about what you are going to say and how you might deal with differing reactions. You'll need to respond to questions with confidence without becoming angry or defensive.

For some people it will not be an issue, others may find your sexuality confronting or scary and it may take them some time to accept it.

Really think it through before you say anything, and choose who you tell wisely. The last thing you want is people gossiping behind your back. Ask yourself:

1. Are you sure you're gay? Can you answer with 100 per cent confidence?
2. If your family or friends' reaction upsets you, do you have someone you can turn to for support?

3. Are you prepared to give your friends and family time to adjust to this new information?

Choose a time when the atmosphere is open and relaxed, and no-one has to rush off anywhere, to tell the people you love.

Dealing with people's reactions

People's reactions can be unpredictable, so be prepared. Mostly, my friends already suspected and were cool with it. My mother said she loved me no matter what and that my happiness was the most important thing, but my father wasn't so accepting. I think he felt responsible and worried about what everyone would think. I knew he'd probably have to work through feelings of shock, maybe even denial. It would take some time before he could accept it.

I didn't flaunt my sexuality because I didn't want to make anyone uncomfortable. At the same time, I didn't hide it either. People became more comfortable about it as time went on; amongst my friends it wasn't such a 'novelty'.

I only had one friend who rejected me. It was hurtful because I'd known her since primary school and we were close growing up. I figured that she knew me as a certain type of person and when I didn't turn out to be that way she couldn't deal with it. Being rejected hurt, but it helped me remember that I am unique and special, and sharing an important part of who I am with the people I love. If they choose to ignore this, they are missing out on knowing who I am.

Carly

What I learned

- I have every right to be who I am.
- My quality of life and levels of happiness improve dramatically when I'm being true to myself.
- If someone doesn't accept me for who I am, they don't deserve to be in my life.
- I learned who my real friends are and I'm so grateful for their love and support.

Carly

Q: WHAT IF MY FAMILY ASKS ME TO LEAVE HOME?

A: Kids Helpline 1800 55 1800 or Lifeline 131 114 will help you find accommodation.

Q: HOW CAN I FIND OUT ABOUT SOCIAL FUNCTIONS AND GROUPS?

A: Pick up a gay and lesbian newspaper. They will have details about events as well as how to access support and social groups. There are also national magazines available.

For more information call the Gay and Lesbian Counselling Service in your state or territory. These services are anonymous and calls to a 1800 number do not appear on a phone bill.

An expert's view

- You cannot predict how others will react so choose carefully who you tell, when and for what outcome you wish for.
- Be very clear yourself as to why you wish to tell someone and make sure it is about you, not about what you want from them; you need to feel good about coming out and that you will be safe doing so no matter what reaction they have.
- Be prepared for any reaction, including responses such as silent shock, 'I already knew', tears, hugs and support, or anger.
- If someone reacts badly, appreciate that their initial reaction may shift to something more supportive once they are past the shock and have had time to take it in.
- When you tell someone, let them know why you have chosen to tell them (for example, to be more real, more honest, freer, to be yourself) and how you would like them to react (just say okay, please keep it to yourself, know I am still the same as yesterday, etc.). This can be very helpful in getting the response you want as often the other party doesn't know how to react even when they do want to be supportive.
- Consider role playing the discussion with a professional or a supportive understanding friend first. You could get help from the Gay and Lesbian Council, Reach Out or a private counsellor specialising in this area.

Tessa Marshall
Director, Marshall Coaching Group

More information
Gay and Lesbian Counselling Service
ACT
Gay and Lesbian Telephone Help Referral and Outreach
Bureau (THROB)—(02) 6247 2726
QLD
Gay and Lesbian Welfare Association—(07) 3252 2997
(7–10 p.m.)
Toll free (rural areas)—1800 184 527
SA
Gay and Lesbian Counselling Service—(08) 8422 8400
(Mon–Fri 7–10 p.m., Sat 2–5 p.m. & 7–10 p.m.)
Toll free (rural areas)—1800 182 233
NSW
Gay and Lesbian Line—(02) 8594 9596 (5.30–10.30 p.m.
daily)
Toll free (rural areas)—1800 184 527
VIC
Gay and Lesbian Switchboard—(03) 9827 8544
(6–10 p.m. daily, Wed 2–10 p.m.)
Toll free (rural areas)—1800 184 527
WA
Youthline—(08) 9486 9855 (Tuesdays 1–4 p.m.)
TAS
Gay and Lesbian Switchboard—1800 184 527

WHAT IF I THINK I'M GAY?

Having feelings for someone of the same sex can be extremely confusing. You may feel very close to someone of the same sex who you already know or find yourself thinking of someone of the same sex who you don't know (such as a celebrity) in a sexual way.

Many people experience these thoughts and feelings, but this doesn't necessarily mean that you're gay.

For example:

- Some people feel this way about someone of the same sex purely because they love and care for them so intensely.
- Some people feel this way because they are curious.
- Some people feel this way because they are attracted to both sexes.
- Some people feel this way because they idolise the person they are attracted to.
- Some people don't trust people of the opposite sex and feel more comfortable with members of their own sex.
- Some people may not feel attracted to members of the opposite sex because this just doesn't feel right to them.

All of these experiences and feelings are natural and many people go through similar times in their lives.

The important things to remember are:

- You are not alone.
- You should not rush into making any decisions (regarding labels etc.).

- There is no need to give yourself a label—you don't need to define yourself as 'gay', 'straight', 'bi' or 'X' if you don't want to.
- There is no right or wrong answer.
- Seek advice and support from a counsellor, friend, family member or youth service. These people may be able to help you to explore your feelings if you are experiencing anxiety, upset, anger, etc.

Charlotte Beaumont-Field

Wellbeing Manager, Inspire Foundation

Advice on coming out

- 'Coming out' is the term usually given to the process when you have made a decision about your sexuality and want to tell someone that you are 'gay', 'bi' or 'lesbian'.
- People often choose to tell someone they know and trust first before they tell larger groups—this is a good idea as usually this person will be supportive and may even help you to let more people know.
- However, even if you are close to and trust the person you decide to tell, they may react in a way that you do not expect. They might feel angry, sad, surprised and maybe even hurt. This may be because they feel that it means the relationship between the two of you could change. It is best to prepare yourself for a range of different reactions and understand that it may take time for the other person to

accept your news or they may not be able to continue the friendship.

- Please seek support and advice from someone—like a counsellor—first and they can help you explore things that you may not have thought about. They can also help you prepare for different reactions that may result from informing others about your sexuality.
- Be true to yourself—it's your life and you need to be honest with yourself and love yourself for who you are.

Charlotte Beaumont-Field

Wellbeing Manager, Inspire Foundation

- A general rule of thumb for seeking professional help is feeling like you need to or wondering if you need to. Also any change in thoughts, feelings and behaviour that is out of character for you might indicate you should talk to a professional.
- Talk to someone you trust—this may be a friend to start with. Or you can go straight to your GP or local counsellor. Remember that you may need to knock on more than one door to get through the right one—hang in there.
- If at any stage the person you've chosen to confide in doesn't take you seriously, and you feel as though you're being dismissed, keep talking to different people. There are always options such as headspace or Lifeline or Kids Helpline.

Vikki Ryall

Clinical Manager, headspace National Office

In profile: Amy

Age: 23

Hair colour: Naturally light brown but purple at the moment!

Eye colour: Blue

Favourite sayings: 'It's all good' and 'Everything happens for a reason'.

Greatest personal moment: Ranking top of Sydney Institute and third state-wide for my Tertiary Preparation Certificate (like HSC). It just proves that you can do anything if you put your mind to it and want it bad enough!

Dream yet to accomplish: To go to Alaska to see the aurora borealis (northern lights)

Favourite colour: Purple

Favourite place in the world: Anywhere that has great open views, especially of mountains or water or both, because it brings about a peace in me that I can't seem to get anywhere else

Best tip: To never give up even when life keeps beating you down

Favourite quote: 'Always dream and shoot higher than you know you can do. Don't bother just to be better than your contemporaries and predecessors. Try to be better than yourself.' *William Faulkner*

Dream for my future: To be happy

POWER STATEMENT

I learned that when I felt strong enough to take myself out of my comfort zone, this is what allowed me to learn and grow and truly embrace life.

Chapter 12

SELF-HARMING—THE PAIN BEHIND THE SCARS

> 👓 Did you know . . .
>
> Some people who engage in self-harming behaviours report that self-harm becomes addictive.[7] It can become their main way to deal with any emotional pain or stressor in their life and they become unable to deal with things in any other way.[8]

Sometimes, in the depths of despair, self-harming can feel like the only way to ease the pain of emotional turmoil. But self-harming is dangerous and can leave you with permanent scars.

If you or someone you know is engaging in self-harming behaviour, it will probably be by:

- cutting the skin with sharp objects such as scissors or knives

- burning the skin with cigarettes or hot objects such as an iron
- sticking pins or toothpicks into a scab or wound
- hitting the body with fists
- grating the skin with objects such as a comb.

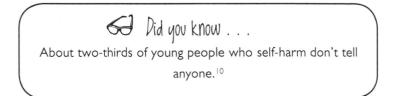

👓 Did you know . . .

If a person has self-harmed before, they have a much higher chance of self-harming again when placed under stress or crisis, or if they experience emotions they're unable to cope with.[9]

Hiding the pain

When people self-harm it can be for a number of reasons. Usually it is a way of coping with overwhelming emotions and dealing with anger, self-hatred or intense sadness. Scars and injuries are kept secret by lying about the cause of the wounds and covering them with clothing or jewellery. Hiding scars is the same as hiding from the underlying cause. But resisting the reasons you want to hurt yourself will not make them go away.

Melinda

👓 Did you know . . .

About two-thirds of young people who self-harm don't tell anyone.[10]

IT FELT LIKE MY ONLY WAY OUT

I hated school. I preferred to spend time on my own, but all the activities I used to enjoy became a chore, and I didn't know what else to do, so I cut myself. This gave me a split-second of release, then I'd feel guilty. I'd think to myself, *You're an idiot.* Then I had the urge to do it again. For me it was having a sense of control over the pain and a momentary escape from the hell of depression. It felt like my only way out. The antidepressants I was prescribed weren't helping so they prescribed me other ones, and the dose kept going up until there was a change in my emotions. I cut myself until after I turned seventeen and still get urges now, but have learned to talk myself out of it.

When I didn't cut I'd take numerous amounts of pills, either Panadol or my own medication. There was one time I tried to overdose on them and was taken to the office at school for my mum to pick me up. This was just another control mechanism, even though I didn't really have control over my body when overdosing because you never know what effect different pills will have on your body. My mum went through my room time after time to dispose of any harmful things, but I still found ways of getting things like razors or Panadol.

Lauren

I SELF-INJURED BECAUSE I YEARNED TO FEEL LOVED

I was ten years old when I started self-injuring. I'd endured a long period of sexual abuse from my father. I can't recall exactly how I felt at the time. The truth is that the early days of hurting myself are hazy.

It's not uncommon for someone to not know exactly why they started, but they know that if it didn't feel good or serve some purpose it would never have continued. I never really felt like I fitted into my family or my skin. I felt angry and alone a lot of the time, and was having strange dreams which I didn't understand; I now know they were flashbacks to the abuse. When I was twelve I was depressed and used to listen to sad music in the dark.

I didn't tell anyone I self-injured. At first I didn't even know how to do it, but I figured it out when I witnessed a girl at school fall over and deeply graze her leg. It wasn't so much the injury itself that got to me, it was all the attention lavished upon her. I felt as though I was invisible and the yearning to feel loved deep within led me to try it out.

The first time I self-injured, I pricked myself with pins on my wrist and fingers. Then I graduated to using nail clippers to take out chunks of flesh.

Self-injuring left marks and scars and I constantly lied about it. I'd say I tripped over, or find some random explanation to keep it a secret. I also became very good at hiding my injuries and the dressings that covered them.

My secret's out

When I was eleven I told the school counsellor, and she told Mum, and my secret was out. But Mum wasn't sure how to deal with it initially. She didn't know how to help. She was convinced that hiding all the sharp implements in the house would stop me, but I found a way anyway.

I used pins with coloured heads to prick my skin. I'd poke the scars, or I'd scratch at them or use nail clippers to take chunks out of the top of my legs. Then I discovered razors and I'd remove the blades and use those. I also used a Stanley knife and glass to cut myself.

I had few scars until I was about thirteen.

Cutting myself was a coping mechanism. If my parents were fighting, it was one way of forgetting my family's problems for a while. I hid my injuries under long skirts and the better I got at it, the more I created a ritual to keep it a secret.

My ritual included keeping the blood contained so it didn't stain the carpet or floor. Sometimes I'd do it in the bathroom and put paper towel underneath. I had a first-aid kit so I could patch up the cuts afterwards. I knew exactly what I was doing and had no plans of stopping.

When my mum confronted me about my scars, I was placed under psychiatric care. I got so comfortable there that I didn't want to leave. So as soon as I was sent home, I self-injured just so I'd be put back in, because home life was heartbreaking and difficult. One day, I became so distraught at the thought of being sent home, I told a staff member that if they made me go back home, I'd kill myself. This was the first time someone took notice of how much pain I was in.

When I was thirteen I was taken into state care. Because there were too many people around who could witness what I was doing, I started self-harming in public toilets and parks to preserve my secret.

When things got really bad, Dad volunteered to move out of the family home so I could move back in. Mum said no. She chose my father over me. Three years later, Dad had an affair and is now married to that woman. I still can't believe Mum chose to protect him over me, given the way he treated her.

Finding freedom again

I went into independent living just after my seventeenth birthday. Dad had money and felt guilty so made a play to win me over: He said he'd pay my rent so I wasn't forced to live in a refuge. Even though he paid my rent, I had no other income, so couldn't properly support myself. I started hanging around the streets and going to local food banks. I met up with a guy I'd known when I was thirteen and living in care. I had always been scared of him. One day, feeling vulnerable, I let him into my house and he raped me.

It took me a week to tell the police. I feared they wouldn't believe me. A close friend insisted I tell the police, so reluctantly

I did. But I refused to press charges out of fear of what this guy might do to me. Instead, I bought a one-way ticket to another state and moved away.

It was the best thing I ever did.

I changed my name, phone numbers and severed all contact with my father. I was in and out of refuges for six months, but nothing could replace the feeling of freedom. I didn't speak to Mum for eight months and told my sister I didn't want any contact with either of my parents for a while. I knew I needed to get my feet on the ground and figure myself out. I began to trust myself and this felt empowering.

I started seeing a counsellor who specialises in sexual abuse, and she was the first person who believed me. This was what helped me get back on track because finally one person believed me without question or judgement.

What helped

Drawing, writing poetry, flicking elastic bands on my wrist all worked to distract me. As I got older I became more disciplined. I realised drinking, smoking and cutting were all linked to coping. When I wasn't cutting, I was drinking. When I stopped drinking, I'd start cutting again.

The more I dealt with the past, the more I learned to control self-injury. With every ounce of energy I'd need to watch myself closely and keep it in check. The longest I've ever gone without self-injuring is six months.

I gave up drinking last year for nine months and that helped a lot with consciously controlling the urges to injure myself.

How to stop self-injuring

Distraction! There is a technique called the fifteen-minute rule—see if you can go fifteen minutes, then another fifteen minutes, and so on. I used TV and would say to myself, *Maybe I'll cut myself after this show.* I tricked myself into passing time so at the end of the night, I couldn't be bothered going to the hospital, and if I'd been drinking I couldn't drive so I'd have to tell someone—it was easier to go to bed.

Amy

If you're self-injuring . . .

- If you can't find someone who will listen, keep on looking. If you have to go to 50 different people until someone listens and believes you, do it. Don't be afraid of what people are going to think.

- If you're happy within yourself, you don't need to worry about what other people think.

- If you see a doctor and they immediately want to put you on medication, perhaps get a second opinion. In my experience, and from the medical journals I have studied for my work in community service, medication is only useful if you actually have a mental illness, such as depression, bipolar, etc. Those who self-injure may not necessarily have an illness that requires medication; however, all self-injury does require professional counselling.

- Establish what your triggers are, and what you get out of self-injuring. The main reason I did it was to cope. It used to be about intense situations—a bad day at school, my parents fighting, or if I said something stupid I shouldn't have. Flashbacks, though, were my main trigger. You are self-injuring for a reason, so pay attention to your feelings. Use distraction, drawing or writing poetry to get your feelings out. This will help you make sense of them.
- Don't self-injure to try to fit into groups. If people don't like you for who you are, they're not your real friends. Self-injury should never be a way to fit in.
- Get more active—something as simple as going for a walk can lift your mood. When I was going to the gym, I felt so much happier. Activity is a way of self-nurturing.

Amy

What to do if you know someone who is self-injuring
Listen to them. Acknowledge their story, even if you can't relate to it. It is very real to the person going through it. Help them to get help, and take them seriously.
Amy

I JUST WANTED TO ESCAPE THE PAIN

When I made the transition from primary to high school, it felt like a monumental change and I found it really hard to deal with. I didn't have many friends and suddenly I felt alone. I didn't fit in and I started to feel anxious all the time. People made fun of me and it was horrible. I fell into a constant state of nervousness and stress and eventually this led to depression.

Those times I felt the most out of control, I'd cut myself with a razor blade. I wanted to feel a release, a different kind of pain to the emotional turmoil that constantly plagued me.

I stopped going out and spent most of my time in my room. The scars from my cuts were visible but no-one seemed to care that I was out of sorts; no-one asked me what was wrong.

I thought it was just me, and that no-one else felt that deep, intense loneliness. There was no-one I felt I could relate to or talk to, and I felt isolated and alone.

Lauren

👓 Did you know . . .

In one study a participant reported that her self-harming behaviours helped her to feel more 'in control', whereas her suicidal behaviour occurred when she felt out of control.[12]

CUTTING MADE ME FEEL IN CONTROL

I was eleven when I started high school and my life revolved around therapy and antidepressants. I was so different to everyone. I had a small group of friends who were a toxic crowd. I started hanging out with people I knew were doing negative things, but I didn't care. I was moody, angry and frustrated. I changed into a negative person. Soon after, I started to pull my hair out whenever I felt like I was going to cry. Whenever I did cry I locked my bedroom door and in the privacy of my own bedroom I would cut my arms until they were bleeding. I couldn't talk about my issues, and this was the only way I felt I could escape for such a long time. This was my coping mechanism, cutting myself made me feel as if I was the one in control.

Veronica

I CRAVED MUM'S LOVE

I started to self-harm from a very young age. The first time I did it I was eight. Mum got angry with me and as I leaned back to get out of the way, I fell and landed on the fireplace. I burnt my hand and found that instead of worrying about Mum's anger, I focused on the pain. This put it in my head that injury was a way to escape pain.

When I was eleven I got really angry and yelled and screamed at Mum, demanding to know why she never spoke to me. I became violent because Mum was always violent with me. I shoved her and then I broke down. Mum told me that what goes on inside a family stays on the inside. She said, 'You never tell anyone outside of the family what is going on behind closed doors.' I believed her because I loved her so much and craved for her to love me too. I thought all families were exactly the same, and that no-one ever shared what really went on inside their family with anyone external.

Between the ages of thirteen and sixteen, I consistently self-harmed once or twice a week. I used anything to hurt myself. I never cut any part of my body that was visible to anyone else. Only ever under my breasts, on my belly or the top of my thighs, places no-one would be able to see.

I always appeared outwardly happy at school. I was an A+ student and worked hard. I wanted everyone to think I was perfect. But that was far from the truth. I self-harmed because I blamed myself for not being the kind of daughter a mother could love. I hated how my mother made me feel. And self-harming was the only way to escape the pain of abandonment.

Worst moment

One time I'd been self-harming and cut all along the side of my body. I'd fallen asleep on my bed when I was supposed to be babysitting my siblings. Mum came home, stood beside my bed and jammed her foot into my side so hard it hurt my stomach. She kicked me over, exposing a big red patch on the sheets where my cut had bled. She looked at the blood, then looked me in the eye, and walked away.

I felt like it was the one time she could have said, 'Why are you doing that?' or 'Please don't do that'. She could have shown me some kind of love. She could have even said, 'You're a stupid girl', and it would have made me happy. I needed her to speak to me and the fact that she just walked away and left me there fed every emotion that made me cut myself, and made it worse.

Stopping my self-harm

Because I wasn't yet sixteen the youth liaison counsellor had to disclose to my parents what was going on in my sessions. I was told that they'd called my dad in and I was terrified because he was finally going to find out that I'd been self-harming and how many years it had been going on.

In that moment I knew I had to stop self-harming. I had my little sister to look after. We were so close and I knew I couldn't protect her from this forever.

I felt massive relief about stopping. After Dad knew, I couldn't physically bring myself to self-harm. I threw out all my pocket knives and even had a friend shave my legs so I wasn't holding a razor blade in my hand.

When I stopped it was the first time I could see with clarity how much self-harm had been ruling my life. It was all I thought about, and everything I did related back to it. I'd even written it into a schedule: 'Between the hours of ten and eleven you can do what you like'—my secret message to myself, giving myself permission to self-harm.

Strategy to stop self-harming

My youth liaison counsellor and I developed a system for when I felt the familiar pang of wanting to hurt myself. It had to do with my hand, and every finger had a meaning that I would recite aloud:

- Thumb = Thumbs up—I know I'm going to be okay. A part of me wants me to be okay and that part is stronger than the part that wants to harm.
- Pointing finger = If Mum made me feel angry, I used to blame it on myself. The pointing finger reminds me to ask whoever has made me angry, as politely as I can, to point out where I'm going wrong.
- Middle finger = If they can't tell me what I'm doing wrong, I'm not doing anything wrong.
- Ring finger = Patience is a virtue I know I possess. Be patient. If something isn't going my way, remember that maybe tomorrow it will be different.
- Little finger = If I still want to hurt myself and don't know what to do, call my counsellor.

Bronte

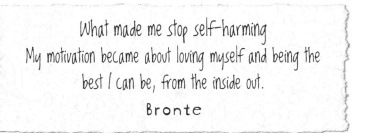

What made me stop self-harming
My motivation became about loving myself and being the best I can be, from the inside out.
Bronte

In profile: Bronte

Age: 18
Hair colour: Brown
Eye colour: Green
Favourite saying: 'Your past doesn't and never will determine your future.'
Greatest personal moment: Working with young people on a camp and helping them to realise and achieve their goals
Dream yet to accomplish: To have all my siblings graduate high school and grow up knowing they are loved; to become a general nurse.
Favourite colour: Purple
Favourite place in the world: 'The Gorge', Airly, Victoria
Best tip: Listen to yourself and believe in who you are. Never let anyone make your decisions; live the life you choose.
Favourite quote: 'Life goes on.'
Dream for my future: To be the best nurse and travel the world

POWER STATEMENT

Don't rely on adults who appear to have all the answers. Rely on the people who have the life experience to help you. Being listened to and understood by someone who knows what you're going through because they've been there is the greatest gift.

An expert's view

WHAT ARE SOME STRATEGIES TO OVERCOME SELF-HARM?

The main intervention is DBT—dialectical behavioural therapy—which represents 'mindfulness emotion regulation'. In other words, being in the moment, completely aware of what is going on around you, and aware of your triggers. A trigger will cause your feelings to build up so it is important to learn how to identify and control those feelings.

Another effective intervention is CBT—cognitive behavioural therapy—which represents a solution-focused approach, establishing the triggers and employing distracting techniques to help shift focus.

TRIGGERS

A trigger is what causes your emotions to suddenly build up to the point where engaging in self-harm helps to manage those tumultuous feelings.

Working out your triggers is crucial to developing ways to overcome the urge to self-injure. A trigger could be a recurring bad memory, a particular time of day (evenings are often a bad time as this is when people find themselves alone, thinking about things), or an argument with your parents, or boyfriend or girlfriend.

The key to overcoming the urge to self-injure is to find alternative ways of dealing with these emotions.

COPING WITH EMOTIONS

Once your triggers are established, consider an alternative approach that helps relieve those feelings. Distraction through creating a similar physical sensation can help to alleviate overwhelming feelings and emotions. Try these:

- snap an elastic band against your wrist
- squeeze ice cubes in your hands
- thrust your arm into a bucket of cold water
- thrash a pillow against a wall
- throw ice against a brick wall hard enough to shatter it
- break sticks
- plunge your fingers into some ice-cream.

These strategies produce an intense sensation that matches the intense emotions that trigger self-harming. These intense emotions are fleeting so creating a similar physical sensation will allow the feelings to pass—without leaving scars.

WHAT DOES THE COUNSELLING PROCESS INVOLVE?

The counselling process aims to solve the *cause* of the problem through establishing what is motivating the behaviour. It also aims to teach resilient strategies through finding a different 'space' emotionally. Once you begin to see that self-injury is not solving the problem, and start to deal with your emotions, the incidence of self-injury will lessen.

WHAT DO I DO WHEN I FEEL THE URGE TO SELF-HARM?

Ask yourself: *How will injuring myself make things better?* Remind yourself that it *doesn't* make things better.

I HAVE A FRIEND WHO SELF-INJURES ON A REGULAR BASIS. HOW CAN I PERSUADE HER TO SEEK HELP?

Talk to your friend and listen to what she has to say. Encourage her to talk about what's really going on. Help her feel understood by being there for her, and suggesting you seek some support together:

- Services like non-government organisations accept self-referrals without parents' involvement.
- Talk to a teacher you trust, or the school counsellor.
- Call Lifeline on 13 11 14.

Getting help is so important. If something is bothering your friend enough to drive them to self-injure, intervention is a necessity. Talking to someone and getting things out in the open will benefit your friend immensely.

Carolyn Rae
Area Co-ordinator Child and Adolescent Mental Health
Area Mental Health
South Eastern Sydney Illawarra Health Service

Have you heard of . . .

Headspace

'headspace centres: someone else to go to'

www.headspace.org.au

I would really like to encourage you to look for help if you feel you need it. And to ask questions or tell the 'helper' if it doesn't feel like it's working. It may feel like you're all alone with your pain; I believe that you don't have to be. You might feel like your friends are the best support you can have, but sometimes someone outside the situation can be really useful.

Vikki Ryall

Clinical Manager, headspace National Office

In profile: Robert

Age: 16

Hair colour: Brownish black

Eye colour: Crystal blue

Favourite saying: 'Cya around!'

Greatest personal moment: Completing the positive mental attitude challenge by breaking my timber board in half with my bare hand during leader's training at Youth Insearch

Dream yet to accomplish: Winning an Oscar or a TV Week Logie Award

Favourite colour: Blue

Favourite place in the world: Double Island, Queensland, because it is so beautiful and relaxing

Best tip: Keep your goals visible.

Favourite quote: 'Imagination is more important than knowledge.' *Albert Einstein*

Dream for my future: To become a very successful actor, well known around the world

POWER STATEMENT

There is always light at the end of the tunnel—keep walking until you're out of the tunnel. You will get there—don't give up.

Chapter 13

PREGNANT AND SCARED

Finding out you're pregnant can be as terrifying as it is unexpected. Suddenly there are a multitude of considerations and 'what ifs' to think about, and a decision to be made. A decision that, no matter what, will have emotional repercussions far and wide. When/how do I tell the father? What if I decide to keep the baby? Do I have the baby and put it up for adoption? If I have an abortion, will I regret it?

Exploring your options

There is much to consider and counselling services are available to discuss your options so you can make an informed decision and the one that is best for you. (See contacts at the end of this chapter.) As you sift through your emotions and consider what decision feels right for you at this stage of your life, it will help to talk to someone. You do not have to go through this alone, so don't be afraid to reach out for help because help is there.

Melinda

I HAD AN ABORTION AND NOW I CAN'T HAVE CHILDREN

People say that grief is grieving over something you've loved for a long time, then lost. But for me, grief is grieving over something you've never had.

I felt safe in my family with my parents, brother and two sisters. We moved around a lot. Dad was always working and hardly ever home.

Dad had a car accident 23 years ago and developed osteoarthritis. As the years went on it got worse. He became very sick when I was fifteen, and was in and out of hospital. He ended up getting his leg amputated and we were devastated.

That same week, someone tried to burn our house down and Mum was diagnosed with cervical cancer. Suddenly everything veered out of control.

I was not coping and started drinking a lot of alcohol and going out all the time to escape from the fear and uncertainty of what the future held.

I was feeling so vulnerable and I went across the road to my boyfriend's house and was crying in his arms, seeking comfort and needing to feel loved. We started making out and he became forceful and pushy and we ended up having sex. I felt that he took advantage of how vulnerable I was feeling. He was stronger than me, and aggressive in terms of what he expected that night. I should have known better because at times he could be controlling, as well as physically abusive.

As a result I fell pregnant.

When I found out, I felt confused and distraught. I was only fifteen years old. What was I going to do?

I told my parents and they told me they were dead against abortion, but said I didn't have much choice. I felt the abortion was forced on me because no-one ever asked me what I wanted, or put forward any other possible option for discussion.

Mum and Dad didn't care how I felt

During the procedure, something went wrong, and as a result, I can't ever have children.

When I had it done, Mum wasn't even there. She left me at the hospital and went and played the pokies. When it was over, she signed the forms but didn't even ask how I felt. She wouldn't let me get counselling because she said I brought it on myself. It was clear she had no empathy for me, and didn't care how distressed I felt, not only about the abortion, but about not ever being able to fall pregnant again.

My parents treated me like dirt afterwards. Mum was horrible. She told my brother and sisters that I had a baby but the doctor killed it and sucked it out with a vacuum. I felt so devastated that she would do this. My brother and sisters were much younger than me, so how could they possibly comprehend what I was going through emotionally? After that they lost respect for me, and would not talk to me.

Mum locked me in my room and shoved pictures under my door of little babies and the abortion procedure. I didn't need to see all that. It was hard enough going through the anguish of losing a possible future.

My parents made it clear they thought I was a murderer. I was so distraught, I ran to my boyfriend's house to get away from them. Dad rang the police and told them that his 15-year-old suicidal daughter had run away. The police spoke to my parents, then came and found me. One of them said, 'You should not go back home for your own health and safety.' Then they took me to my nan's place.

Nan hugged me and told me everything would be alright. She took me in even though Dad rang and told her, 'You're as good as dead to me'. He won't let her see her grandchildren because he holds a grudge against Nan for helping me. I can't believe my parents hate me that much that they'd rather see me on the streets than living in the safety and comfort of Nan's place.

I realise my dad is going through a lot. He hasn't dealt with his own problems. He spent his childhood in boys' homes and lost his leg at 33 years old. Mum also had an awful childhood and hasn't dealt with her issues either.

Mum's sister had an abortion when she was eighteen, so I thought Mum would be more understanding of my situation. She was supportive of her sister but not of me.

It hurts to think they don't love me or want me around, and have poisoned my brother and sisters against me.

Cruelty pushed me over the edge

To make matters worse, people were so cruel. They'd drive past my house and throw baby dolls at it. At school people would say things like, 'Katie's a murderer, she killed her baby.'

Someone put a voodoo doll in my locker with knives sticking out of it, and a note that said, 'This is your baby'. Someone else bombarded my inbox with emails that had links to baby-related websites.

It was all so upsetting that I had to leave school.

When I started at Tafe, studying for a Children's Services Diploma, I thought it would be a fresh start. But then people said things like, 'Why should you work with kids, you'd probably just kill them.'

I felt so alone. I lost respect for myself and had no self-esteem. I started self-harming, and drinking every night to the extent that I'd wake up in gutters. One time I woke up an hour from where I lived with no idea how I got there.

I ploughed through social workers and hated them all. The very nature of their questions made me feel angry. I didn't want their help, and thought I didn't need it.

Turning it around

I attended a youth camp and spoke openly for the first time about what I was feeling inside. It felt good to be listened to without judgement, and to be supported and nurtured.

I felt so ashamed for what I did. I thought people would be more understanding, but instead they were cruel.

Talking about what happened made me realise that counselling would help me deal with it and move on. So I found a new social worker and, as a result, I really do feel as though I've faced it and waded through the pain and guilt to the other side.

Katie

✍

More information
Kids Helpline: www.kidshelp.com.au
Phone: 1800 55 1800
Sexual Health & Family Planning Australia:
www.shfpa.org.au

An expert's view

WHAT IF YOU THINK YOU'RE PREGNANT?

Prevention

Prevention is always the best option. Use contraception and don't feel like you can't say no if your partner will not use a condom.

Know your body

Get to know your body so that you recognise changes in it. If you're pregnant, sometimes even before getting a positive reading on a home pregnancy test, you will get signs such as sore breasts, puffiness, needing to urinate more often (especially during the night) and just feeling 'different'.

Get tested

If you think you might be pregnant, buy a couple of test kits at a pharmacy and follow the instructions. If it is positive, you can also get a blood test confirmation either via your doctor or, if you're worried about your family doctor knowing, you can ring your local community health centre or family planning clinic for further testing. Privateclinic.com.au is also a good resource.

Talk to someone

Deciding what to do if you're pregnant can be very emotional and difficult. Ultimately it's your decision whether now is the right time for you to have a child and take on the enormous responsibility of becoming a parent. Community health nurses, family planning clinics and pregnancy helplines are all there to assist you confidentially with making this decision (be aware that some are affiliated to specific churches or philosophies and therefore may not be totally impartial). If you feel safe to, you could also talk to your parents and/or your partner or a trusted friend about what to do.

Get help

Know that you're not alone despite this being a very lonely time. Recognise that you don't need to feel ashamed or embarrassed. Do not hesitate to reach out for help as it is there.

Tessa Marshall

Director, Marshall Coaching Group

In profile: Katie

Age: 17

Hair colour: Brown-ish

Eye colour: Blue

Favourite saying: 'Silly 'lil pumpkin'

Greatest personal moment: Having the opportunity to be a part of Youth Insearch and all the experiences it holds; meeting with the Australian Minister of Youth and Victorian Minister of Youth

Dream yet to accomplish: Walk the Kokoda Trail

Favourite colour: Purple

Favourite place in the world: Blue pools; I used to sit by the water and throw rocks into it to release stress

Best tip: Stay positive

Favourite quote: 'If this is the worst thing that happens today, I'll be okay.'

Dream for my future: To work with children and be happy in all I do; to give as much as I can and be a role model to as many people as possible

POWER STATEMENT

You can only make a decision based on what you know in the moment.

Chapter 14

COPING WITH BULLYING

👓 Did you know . . .
Children who are bullied are more likely to have higher levels of stress, anxiety, depression and illness.[13]

It's hard enough to feel confident at the best of times and almost impossible if you're a victim of bullying. Bullies will try to undermine your self-esteem by intimidating you and often recruit other people to join in. The great news is that many schools now have anti-bullying policies in place, which means it's getting easier to stop bullies in their tracks.

The bully is the problem

Bullying is exerting power over another person by calling them names, saying nasty or threatening things, ignoring them, leaving them out or making them feel uncomfortable or frightened. Bullies are usually trying to be popular or wanting to appear tough and in control. Some bullies may not even understand that their behaviour is wrong.

You have a right to feel safe and secure so if you're being bullied, tell your parents or someone in a position of authority who can do something to protect you. Remember, you are not the problem—the bully is.

Melinda

TAKING A STAND

Don't be afraid to stand up to a bully. These people are insecure so if you stand up to them, usually they will back down. One of the girls who bullied me at school said, when I walked into the bathroom, 'There's an earthquake coming'. Tired of her constant taunts about my weight, I turned to her and said, 'Stop it and shut up'. I stood up to her and she left me alone after that and everyone else did too.

Lauren

I was bullied at times and there was a period where I became a bully too. I'd sense weakness in someone else and intimidate them. I think this was driven by a need to be accepted, and have some sort of influence or control in my life.

Tom

Because I came from a sheltered Christian school, and kept to myself, I didn't have any people or social skills. Moving from a sheltered environment into a public school where everyone had attitude was a big shock. I didn't fit in and was constantly bullied. I felt alone during the process of changing schools, because I had no-one to guide me. I hated school and it was a horrible time.

Alexis

I was probably about seven or eight when I had just moved from a different area in the suburbs with a different culture of people. I grew up with an Islamic background, so I didn't really connect with many of the kids at my school. I got bullied because I was chubbier than most of the girls at school. I'd come home and be surrounded with adults. Growing up I felt like I didn't belong. My family didn't understand the loss that I was feeling; in little over five years my once happy life turned into a life that I felt I was living alone.

Veronica

DEATH STARTED A DOWNWARD SPIRAL

A few years ago, I contracted golden staph disease. It started in my knee and the infection spread to my scalp. My scalp bled and my hair became matted with blood, so I was forced to shave my head. Because I looked different and had an obvious illness, people at school bullied me. They made fun of the scars on my scalp and teased me about dying. This made me feel hopeless and I found it hard to make friends and fit in. I became very depressed.

My grandfather had to have his voice box removed because he had throat cancer. Although he could still be understood with the help of a special vibrating device, it was hard on the family and a lot to deal with on top of my golden staph.

A few months later my nan passed away. I was really close to her and her death hit me hard. On top of this, my stepfather took my younger brother interstate and he started telling lies that my other brothers and I had been abusing him. My stepfather was a trouble-maker and made a big deal about it. Mum was devastated.

Eventually (after having golden staph) my hair grew back and this helped my confidence, but then my pop passed away from liver cancer. My younger brother couldn't come back for the funeral due to my stepfather and this upset the family.

Around this time I started to feel that my world was closing in around me and my depression worsened.

My mum moved us out of the city, to the country, so we could have a fresh start.

I was a bit apprehensive about my new school because I didn't know anyone. I started in term two and made a few friends. One of the teachers was really strict. One time, when I ruled a margin, she insisted it was crooked and I had to do it again. It looked straight to me, so I challenged her and she ordered me out of the classroom. Her taunting me became a regular occurrence until I got to the point where I felt I couldn't take it anymore. I saw the principal and deputy principal and told them what happened, hoping it would make a difference to her classroom behaviour. But it didn't, and her verbal abuse got worse.

I felt so helpless. Because even the principal knew what was going on and had done nothing to stop it, I felt I had no choice but to take the matter into my own hands. So I sent two email bomb threats to the school for the periods I had this teacher. The school took them seriously and the police became involved. I felt scared but the damage was done. They tracked the email back to me and I was taken to the police station for questioning.

My reputation was damaged

I explained to the police my reasons for sending the emails. As it turned out, there were previous events like this directly related to this teacher. I was given an official caution and let go. I felt so relieved I hadn't been formally charged. It made me think about my behaviour, and how terrified I'd felt when I got caught and how badly it could affect my future. I knew I'd never do anything like that again.

But the event permanently marred my reputation. Everyone knew it was me who had done the bomb threats. My friends dropped me. People in the 'bad' crowd asked me to do bomb threats for them, to get them out of certain classes. I became popular among the bad crowd, but not in a positive way. The bullying became worse and I was relentlessly made fun of.

I desperately wanted to go back to the city, back to my old school, to everything that was familiar and safe. But Mum was settled in the country. Although she suffered depression, she was happy in her job and she didn't want to move us again.

With Mum depressed and helpless, I grew even more distant from everyone and everything. I felt so alone. I missed my younger brother, and my nan and pop. But at the time I felt no-one seemed to notice that I was struggling, or how far out of it I felt.

I was suspended for twenty days for making the bomb threats, so my mother sent me to another school. But as it was a small town, everyone there knew about it and the bullying became unyielding.

I was branded a trouble-maker and no-one cared what had driven me to the point of helplessness. Or that I felt taking action to get myself out of that class was my only option. If someone had looked deeper, they would have seen a confused teenage boy whose self-esteem had been chipped away until there was nothing left.

Breaking point

My breaking point came when my maths teacher made me look stupid in front of the whole class. I'm not that great at maths and when he asked me a question I couldn't answer, he said, 'That's not the way you do it, you idiot.'

I had wanted to take the maths problem home and show my tutor so he could help me with it. But the teacher said I had to do it there. Halfway through the class I packed up my stuff and left. I felt like I didn't belong there, that I didn't belong anywhere.

I went to see the deputy principal, ready to yell and scream. But I didn't want to get into any more trouble. So instead, I decided to kill myself. I found a high wall and jumped off.

I was paralysed for a few days and during that time all I could think about was how lost I felt.

Inspired by leaders

I went on a youth camp and this is where I learned that I had a vivid imagination which I needed to tame, and if I could do that, I could use it to my advantage to achieve my dream of becoming an actor, producer and writer.

I was so inspired by the leaders at the youth camp, and their courage and strength, that I wanted to become a youth leader. I worked hard to complete my stage 1 and 2 leaders' training.

During this time, the founders of the youth program, Ron and Judith Barr, could see my passion for acting and wanted to help me. Ron took me to The Australian International Performing Arts High School (AIPAH) and I auditioned. I loved the vibe of the school and knew it was an amazing opportunity. I was elated when I was accepted.

What should you do if you're being bullied?

If you're being bullied by a fellow student, talk to teachers and your parents until your voice is heard.

If you're being bullied by a teacher, if no-one at the school will listen or take the appropriate action, talk to your parents and ask them to talk to the school and insist that something be done. If this doesn't work, go with your parents to the police.

Robert

Because I was new and didn't really fit in, I was bullied at
school. My peer group taunted me and made no secret of the
fact that they hated my guts. I was 'the girl with the dead
dad'. Many of my peer group were in my class, which was
terrifying. They stalked me, called me names and beat me up.
Whenever I'd tell someone what had happened in a desperate
attempt to stop the bullying, they'd all cover for each other,
so I looked like the liar. It was so hard, I gave up.

Eventually, after about four years, they stopped. I think it
wasn't fun anymore because the same thing happened every
time. And because we were that much older, I think they
started to realise that what they were doing wasn't okay.

Bullies have self-esteem issues—the only reason they
torment people is because they need to feel good about
themselves. To deal with bullies, ignore them and walk away. If
that doesn't work, or it gets worse, tell someone. Don't give up
and let it continue because you're scared of what will happen
if you tell someone. Speak up and make sure it is dealt with.
The worst thing you can do is cry in front of them, as this
shows that they have succeeded in making you feel bad and
will fuel them to keep teasing you.

Jasmin

Tip

When someone says something nasty, let the words fall in the space between you.

I grew up in a family that looked perfect from the outside, but wasn't always so great on the inside. My dad was emotionally abusive and made me feel as though nothing I did was good enough. As a result I suffered self-esteem issues.

I didn't like school and didn't want to be there. I was bullied constantly and felt as though there was nothing I could do except either ignore it or put up with it in the hope that it would stop.

I started to feel out of place and alone in my situation. I realised that help wasn't going to come looking for me; I had to go looking for it. So I sought counselling and started opening up about being bullied and how helpless I was feeling.

Counselling helped me offload my insecurities and see things for what they were. I was able to gain a different perspective, and realise who I am and what I'm about. I learned that there is always someone out there to help you. But you have to seek it out yourself and be open to it.

James

I was physically and verbally bullied in years 8 and 9. I felt so alone and as though I didn't belong. It was a time of hardship and I felt confused about how to handle it. Eventually I reported it to the school. They helped me by talking to the two people who bullied me and they backed off.

If you are being bullied, try to rise above it and ignore it. Most of the time if you don't react the bullies will get bored and leave you alone. If it gets out of control, report it—tell your parents and the school so that people are aware and can do something about it.

Marcus

A bully is trying to invoke fear. If I'd bought into the fear and kept quiet, they would have continued to bully me and other students, and get away with it. But eventually, because a few of us spoke out, the bullies were expelled and this gave me enormous satisfaction that justice had been done.

James

My brother Jeremy has obsessive compulsive disorder. At primary school he made a bad name for himself because he was always causing trouble.

When I started primary school I became known as 'Jeremy's little brother' or 'that idiot's little brother'. I felt as though I didn't have an identity of my own and everyone had already made up their minds that I would be exactly like Jeremy.

I was bullied because of Jeremy's reputation. My way of dealing with it was to close up and not retaliate. Because of the bullying, and the fact that I kept to myself, I had trouble making friends. It was a lonely, confusing time when all I wanted was to be seen for who I was and to be accepted.

Thankfully my parents sent me to a different high school to Jeremy and that's when I started to come out of my shell. I'm fortunate—I come from a good, loving family and that foundation has helped me to build self-confidence.

Bullying happens a lot at my school, although not to me because now I've learned how to deal with bullies. I try to use my experience to help other people who are being bullied.

Simon

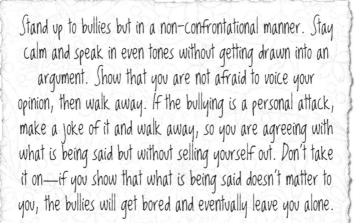

Stand up to bullies but in a non-confrontational manner. Stay calm and speak in even tones without getting drawn into an argument. Show that you are not afraid to voice your opinion, then walk away. If the bullying is a personal attack, make a joke of it and walk away, so you are agreeing with what is being said but without selling yourself out. Don't take it on—if you show that what is being said doesn't matter to you, the bullies will get bored and eventually leave you alone.

Simon

An expert's view

WHAT IS BULLYING?

When one person uses power over another inappropriately and disrespectfully, it is bullying. It can take the form of verbal, physical, emotional or cyber abuse and can include ridiculing, name-calling, teasing, sabotaging, spreading rumours, hitting, recruiting others to help gang-up, etc. Often it's covert rather than out in the open and can be extremely insidious and hard to prove.

Bullies will often try to trivialise or minimise their actions or make out that it's the victim's fault, especially if caught out. They might say:

- 'It was just a bit of fun.'
- 'I was only teasing.'
- 'You can't take a joke.'
- 'You started it.'
- 'Such and such put me up to it.'

WHAT TO DO?

Prevention is the first step.

Where you can, remove yourself from the situation and/or ignore the bully—this can take the fun and power out of it for them. If you don't react, bullies often get bored.

Where you can't remove yourself, you can try the following:

- Assert yourself—Say that the behaviour is not okay. (However, often this won't be enough to get bullies to change. Sometimes it helps to talk to the less aggressive side-kicks rather than the ring leader and they might influence the main bully.)
- If it isn't physical, visualise the bully looking silly (wearing no clothes) to distract yourself from their actions.
- If it's physical, try to prevent getting in situations where you are alone and vulnerable. Recruit your friends to support you, tell trustworthy friends that you need their help. Ask your parents or siblings if you can. If you know a teacher, counsellor or older student who you can trust, ask for their help also. Sometimes it is just not possible to solve it on your own, but you will be amazed how much less of a burden it becomes when you share with others.
- Get professional support via websites such as Reach Out, Kids Helpline, Lifeline or headspace.

Tessa Marshall

Director, Marshall Coaching Group

In profile: James

Age: 16

Hair colour: Black

Eye colour: Brown

Favourite saying: 'Okay, what the bloody hell is going on?'

Greatest personal moment: Being able to help others

Dream yet to accomplish: Lead a trek on the Kokoda Trail

Favourite colour: Black

Favourite place in the world: Double Island, Queensland, because it's the perfect place to relax

Best tip: Only put in what you want in life

Favourite quote: 'When the power of love overcomes the love of power the world will know peace.' *Jimi Hendrix*

Dream for my future: To be one of the top journalists in the country

POWER STATEMENT

Think positively, act positively, live life to the max and don't ever give up no matter how hard it is.

Chapter 15

CYBERBULLYING—HARASSMENT AT A NEW LEVEL

> 👓 Did you know . . .
>
> A quarter of school children experience cyberbullying and some victims don't report incidents to their teachers for fear of losing access to new technologies.[15]

Cyberbullying means teasing and making fun of someone, spreading rumours or sending unwanted messages, either via mobile phone or online. It happens using phones or the internet to create and send harassing or humiliating messages and images. Mean comments, embarrassing photos and videos can be spread through instant messaging, phone texting and by posting on social networking sites.

The anonymity means people who normally would shy away from face-to-face confrontations become bold because they can hide behind their computer or phone.

Hurtful information posted on the internet can be difficult to remove and can be seen by millions of people. However, there are things you can do to keep yourself safe from cyberbullying.

Melinda

👓 Did you know . . .

Cyberbullying is more prevalent in older children with a third of 14–17 year olds reporting that they have been cyberbullied, compared to one in five 10–13 year olds.[16]

Phone safety tips

- Only give your phone number to people you trust in your circle of friends.
- Never give your phone number to someone if you feel you don't want them to have it.
- You can hide your number by setting it to 'private' in the 'settings' section of your phone.

Internet safety tips

- Don't tell your password to anyone. Keep it secret. If you tell one person, they could tell another and someone could go online pretending to be you, or write nasty things on your online profiles.

- Think before you reveal. If you don't want something to go public, don't post it. What you put up on the internet can easily be sent around, and once it's out there you have no control.
- Use the privacy settings in your social networking sites.
- Treat others how you would like to be treated.
- Remember, anything you do online is tracked, and can be traced.
- Use a disposable free email address such as hotmail or gmail. If someone starts harassing you online, you can easily delete the email. You can forward the incoming mail from here to your regular email address.

HOW TO SET UP A DISPOSABLE EMAIL ADDRESS

1. Go to www.gmail.com and sign up.
2. Once you've set up your gmail address, click on the 'Settings' button in the top right corner, and go to the 'Forwarding and POP/IMAP' tab.
3. Select 'Forward a copy of incoming mail to . . .', and enter your other email address.
4. Click 'Save Changes' at the bottom of the page.

All emails sent to the gmail address will automatically be forwarded to your regular email address.

I WAS STALKED ONLINE

My friends and I use chat rooms all the time because they're great for socialising. I got to know this guy who seemed really nice. I loved our online conversations. We had so much in common and talked about anything and everything including movies, music and the merits of charity work. I started to really like him so I gave him my email address. Our chats continued as normal for about a week until suddenly he started asking me very personal questions about sex. I felt so uncomfortable that I ended up blocking him.

But then he bombarded my email inbox with dirty messages and graphic pictures of himself naked. I felt shocked and disgusted. When I replied asking him to stop, his messages became abusive.

I panicked and told my parents and they contacted my ISP and changed my email address. But then I started getting creepy text messages from an unknown number saying things like 'Start looking over your shoulder' and 'I'm watching you'. I was really distressed to the point where I wouldn't leave the house.

My parents reported it to the police, who uncovered a page on the local sports centre website where I do volunteer work that listed my mobile number in connection with a movie charity night I was involved with.

Thankfully once the police intervened and I changed my number, that guy never bothered me again. I realised that I needed to stay anonymous online to protect myself and that included having a user id that is not my real name and being careful not to post personal information.

Jennifer

CYBERBULLIED BECAUSE OF A 'FRIEND'

I became close friends with Erin, the new girl in our class and for a while we were inseparable and shared everything including all our secrets. I gave her my MSN username and password, and didn't think anything of it at the time because I trusted her.

Six months later we had a huge fight and I was really upset. I sent her a few texts that night but she didn't reply.

The next day when I got to school, no-one would talk to me. My group of friends ignored me and I wandered the corridors alone, confused and upset.

I came home to heaps of emails, some from names I didn't even recognise, saying all these awful things like 'I thought you were nice but you're really an evil bitch'. I started to feel bewildered and frightened because I had no idea what was going on. I contacted my ISP to see if they could help me and they put a spam filter on my account so I could only receive emails from the people in my address book.

Then I started getting text messages from unknown numbers saying things like 'Everybody hates you' and 'Why don't you f**k off'. I told my parents what was going on and they called the police, who were able to trace the numbers back to the offenders. The police paid them a visit to issue a warning and discovered I had supposedly sent all my friends a nasty 'group' email revealing certain secrets about them. Reeling in disbelief, I realised what must have happened. Erin must have logged on to MSN with my details and sent my friends a message from me with all the secrets I'd confided to her. I felt devastated. It shattered my confidence to the point where I just wanted to disappear.

I should never have given my personal details to someone else no matter how much I trusted them at the time.

Fiona

MY IDENTITY WAS STOLEN

I'm always downloading free stuff on my computer like games and music, but one day, after downloading a program, my computer became really slow. It took forever to load pages and send emails and whenever I went online there were all these pop-up messages to the point where my computer crashed and I'd have to reboot it.

Then I realised someone else was using my internet banking. My parents called in a tech expert who told us that my computer was infected with spyware, which had screened my online activity to find out my usernames and passwords. Apparently this program is hidden inside free programs downloaded from the internet.

I had to contact my bank and ISP and change my account details and my passwords.

Now I'm so careful about what I download and if I ever get an email from an unknown source I delete it straight away. It's scary how easy it can be for someone to hack into your personal information.

David

More information
http://www.cybersmart.gov.au/en/Teens.aspx

An expert's view

DEALING WITH BULLYING AND CYBERBULLYING—THE IMPORTANCE OF SCHOOLS INITIATING POLICIES

Within the community there is respect, choice and negotiating relationships, and the same principles apply in the school community.

At SCEGGS students are educated in year meetings about managing and negotiating relationships. There are also formal addresses by the principal to ensure students are aware that disrespectful behaviours, including bullying and intimidating, are choices that will not be tolerated within this school community and the appropriate action will be taken.

Every two years students are asked to provide written and anonymous feedback on a range of aspects of school life, including witnessing, hearing about or being subject to a range of disrespectful behaviours. The survey also asks what students do if they are aware of a peer being bullied, cyber or otherwise.

If bullying is identified, intervention is immediate and the behaviour is investigated internally. If an incident is deemed to be serious, the parents are contacted and the issue is discussed. It is then decided which interventions, such as discipline, counselling or expulsion, is appropriate. If a criminal code has been breached, the police may be alerted.

In some cases the perpetrator is someone outside the school and in this instance, once traced back, the link needs to be established to ensure that intervention targets all the individuals involved.

Parents and schools need to assist children by educating them and supporting them to make positive choices in how they manage their relationships, how to say no and how to stand up for themselves and for their friends and colleagues.

Margaret Condonis

School Counsellor, SCEGGS Darlinghurst

What to do if you are being cyberbullied

No-one deserves to be bullied either in the schoolyard or in cyberspace. Prevention is the first step:

- Don't do it to others.
- Only give your phone number and cyber details to trusted friends.
- Don't accept friend invitations or invitations to dialogue with people you don't know and trust.
- Set boundaries around when you will have your phone or computer on and only respond to friendly communications.

If you are being cyberbullied:

- Don't retaliate as this may escalate the situation.
- If you can, ignore any unfriendly communications. Often bullies get bored when they don't get a reaction.
- If something can't be ignored. you have three choices:

- Confront the bully and let them know this is not okay. Ideally have a witness with you when you do this. Be specific and use non-labelling, non-judging language. 'I feel . . . when you . . . because . . .'
- If they don't agree to stop or if you don't feel comfortable confronting them, which is quite common, tell a trusted friend—a problem shared with someone you trust helps take the sting out of it, so talking about it can help you feel less picked on.
- If it becomes a pattern and they won't stop, then you need to speak to someone in authority who has the power to create consequences—parent, teacher, school counsellor, senior prefect. Try and think beforehand what you would like that person to do to help you, but they will also probably have ideas and suggestions that you haven't thought of.

Tessa Marshall

Director, Marshall Coaching Group

Have you heard of . . .
Life Changing Experiences Foundation
SISTER2sister Program
www.lifechangingexperiences.org

The SISTER2sister Program takes in up to 50 at-risk teenage girls per year per program along with their respective Big Sister mentors.

Each of the girls is assigned a Big Sister mentor from the professional community as a positive female role model to provide support, guidance and inspiration where needed, throughout the twelve-month program.

The Big Sister mentors attend a comprehensive training course before being 'matched' with their Little Sister to equip them with the skills and information that will enable them to better assist the needs of their Little Sister.

The program runs risk management workshops and independent living skills seminars. It also teaches goal setting and achieving techniques, and self-coaching strategies. At the end of the program, the girls are equipped with the knowledge and skills to help them break the cycle of trauma and/or abuse and create the future they want.

Many of the girls who have gone through the mentoring program demonstrate an increased level of self-esteem, and confidence in themselves and their abilities to have greater control over their lives and futures. They are able to deal with the effects of their past trauma, develop positive new relationships, demonstrate high self-worth and identify goals and the steps to implement and achieve these goals.

Every girl in the program is a success story waiting to be written. Since the program first began, we have guided and supported more than 150 girls, who have gone on to achieve high school completion, university scholarships and apprenticeships. The girls have demonstrated a dramatic decrease in substance abuse and unplanned teenage pregnancies, and an increase in the continuation of education. More importantly, the program has contributed to the education of the wider community on the issues that affect teenagers at risk.

Jessica Brown
Founder and CEO

It took a few months to establish a respected relationship with my Big Sister. That's when I started to listen and be open to what she was telling me. I found it to be an empowering experience. SISTER2sister helped me gain confidence.

Alexis

During my ordeals I was participating in the SISTER2sister program. I had a Big Sister called Lisa and I couldn't have asked for anyone better. We joked, laughed and talked about everything. I never had an older role model. She was so good to talk to and helped me put things into perspective. We had some amazing experiences together, including climbing the Sydney Harbour Bridge, going whitewater rafting, and I also got to be a back-up singer for Amy Pearson! SISTER2sister was a positive experience.

Veronica

Life Changing Experience's personal message to young people facing hardship

The SISTER2sister ode has become a bit of a mantra for all of us and I hope that any young person facing hardship can take something away from it with them.

Jessica Brown

I must deal with the past yet focus on the future.
I will accept the things I cannot change and change the things I can.
I will deal with my past but focus on my future as whatever I focus on will grow.
I will respect myself by keeping the company of those who respect me.
I will surround myself with positive people who inspire me to be the best I can be.
I will hold my values high and will not let the influences of others change them.
I will not partake in any actions that are not in line with my values,
because I would not be being true to myself.
It is my responsibility to protect myself from harm's way and, when in need of support,

I will turn to those I trust and can do something about it.

Everything I do each day is my own choice.

I will take the time each day to nurture myself by looking after my health.

I am the one who is responsible to look after me.

I am a walking success story waiting to be written. I will start writing it each day.

I will strive to be the best I can be in everything I do.

I will get out of my comfort zone to build up my confidence.

I will take time to smell the roses and be grateful for what I have.

I will create a 'safe place' for myself to deal with the past.

In profile: Alyssa-Kate

Age: 16

Hair colour: Brunette with a reddy-purple tinge through it

Eye colour: Bright green

Favourite saying: 'If life gives you lemons, make lemonade.' 'Turn your negatives into positives.'

Greatest personal moment: If somebody extends their hand out to me for help, I enjoy being the person to help guide them or answer their question; even if I don't have the exact answer they are looking for, I still love that satisfaction of helping another person.

Dream yet to accomplish: To completely achieve my version of success—I'm excited every step of the way

Favourite colour: Rainbow

Favourite place in the world: Anywhere peaceful and tranquil (around nature) where I can sit in awe, meditate and collect/create thoughts; better still, to share that experience with somebody I love

Best tip: Don't go wasting your time hating others. Life is too short to spend time on the negatives.

Favourite quote: 'Plant your own garden and decorate your own soul, instead of waiting for someone to bring you flowers.' *Veronica A. Shoffstall*, 'After a While', 1971

Dream for my future: To become a successful Youth Insearch leader, the best mother, wife and teacher/school counsellor that I can be—in general to be the best I can be and create the future I have always dreamt of for myself

POWER STATEMENT

I don't see myself as a victim nor was I a sufferer of any kind. I'm grateful for what happened, for without it I wouldn't be the person I am today, or have the experiences I have had to help others.

Chapter 16

WHEN DEATH SNATCHES A FRIEND

The loss of a friend feels as though there is a massive hole in your world that can't ever be filled again. Pain, grief and sadness all seem to come in waves, some more intense than others, and at times it can feel overwhelming.

Dealing with grief

Grief doesn't come with a set of rules, or a timeframe in which you're 'supposed' to feel better. Grief is largely unpredictable. It is a process of adjustment and the loss becomes something that you learn to manage.

My heart goes out to you if you've lost someone special. In sharing these stories, I want you to know that you are not alone—other people's hearts have been touched by someone amazing, only to lose them too soon.

Melinda

That's the song his parents played at his funeral and every time I think about my friend that song floods my head. I can remember every single event of the day I found out. It was a beautiful summer evening when I sat down to a barbecue with my family, then the phone rang. As usual I raced my sister to the phone only to be beaten once again. She picked it up and it was for me anyway.

On the other end was my best mate, sounding very down. I asked him what was wrong only to find out that one of our closest friends had taken his own life. *What?* No he didn't . . . this joke is not funny. But after talking more, reality hit me hard. Rohan is dead. I will never go to the movies with him again, I will never play a game of 'b' ball on his front driveway with him again, and never work on his car again.

Was it my fault, were there some signs I missed? Why would he do this to me? We had planned stuff. This just wasn't fair! I felt intense feelings of anger, guilt, remorse and hate. My life did a total backflip. I quit footy, my grades dropped and I stopped hanging out with my friends.

After two months, with my life slowly slipping away, my family and friends took it upon themselves as their duty to get my life back on track. I started talking with them and my intense feelings of anger, guilt, remorse and hate slowly died down. I was amazed that just by talking about my problems with other people, I could start to get my life back on track. Although the feelings were gone I still was very depressed. My parents suggested I talk with a youth worker, which didn't seem to help a bit. My brother then found Reach Out and told me all about it, so with this in mind I read some of the stories and some interviews and realised that I was not the only one who had gone through this. They helped me to realise that there was a light at the end of the tunnel and that I could get through this. Now with my life back on track I definitely have to thank my friends and my family.

Anonymous

A SMILE CAN CHANGE EVERYTHING

I was out with my girlfriends at our usual hotspot on a Thursday night when I found out one of my close friends had committed suicide. I'd lost contact with her when she dropped out of school. We used to vent to each other all the time; we cried together; we were each other's rock. No matter how depressed I was I made sure I had time for others who felt like I did. Her death made me realise how serious depression is. Living with it for the majority of my teenage life, there were times I thought I wouldn't make it to my sixteenth birthday, but I did. It upsets me that I wasn't there for her. Sometimes all it takes is one random act of kindness and it could brighten someone's mood. Days when I felt like it was all too much, little miracles like a random person smiling at me, or seeing other people helping others, turned my day around. I say to myself, as long as I can make one person smile a day, that's 365 people in a year that I might have had a slight impact on.

Veronica

In profile: Justin

Age: 16

Hair colour: Dark brown

Eye colour: Brown

Favourite saying: 'I like pie and pie likes me.'

Dream yet to accomplish: Go skydiving in Hawaii

Favourite colour: Black

Favourite place in the world: Russia—I love their culture and lifestyle

Best tip: Good memories can save your life.

Dream for my future: Be a millionaire

POWER STATEMENT

Good memories can save your life.

I LOST MY BEST FRIEND

When my best friend killed herself, it shook my world. Two weeks before that, she confided to me that her parents were forcing her to take drugs. I wish I could have done something to help her. It was a horrible time and the grief and sadness I felt was overwhelming.

Justin

MY FRIEND WAS BEATEN TO DEATH

James was only fifteen when he was beaten to death in a gang incident. The kids who did it had no personal knowledge of who he was, which hurt the most. He had just arrived at the party after leaving his younger brother's thirteenth birthday party. They were doing it in a sad attempt to get into a gang as they were told they weren't tough enough by the other members.

What made it worse was that the guys who did it were locals. Nice kids who I always thought of as harmless and innocent. I just couldn't believe that the people I knew so well could be capable of doing something like that to someone we loved.

It was a very weird feeling and took about a week to sink in. When it first happened, I felt as though I was in shock. I wanted to call James in the hope that he'd answer the phone, even though a part of me knew he wouldn't. I felt spaced out, as though I was on a high but of the worst possible kind. My whole body felt limp and I couldn't think about anything else. The only time I could find peace was when I was asleep, but after the incident that wasn't very often.

A lot of us didn't talk to each other about how we were feeling, which was probably the worst thing we could have done. We needed to pull together and be there for each other and talk, but instead we separated to try and sort it out in our own way.

Only one person owned up to it and took the blame. The others decided that since they were older, they would have gone to gaol, so they pinned it on the younger one. He took it well and tried to cover for the others, but the evidence on James's body showed three different shoes. The young boy had trouble explaining that to the police, and said that other people must have come along after he'd left. Because no-one else came forward, there wasn't enough evidence to press any charges, so nothing could be done.

Desperate for revenge

A group of us who knew who'd been involved were enraged that they got off so lightly and started plotting revenge.

A counsellor came to the school and sat down with us all. She explained that if we killed the kids who killed James, we're just as bad as they are, and the pain and struggle we and his family are going through would happen to two families, and then someone will take revenge on us and it would keep going. It made us realise what we were thinking of doing was wrong, and not the answer.

The counsellor suggested we start a campaign so something positive could come out of James's death. So we helped start the 'One punch could kill' campaign to raise awareness that what someone might think is an innocent punch could end up killing someone.

I've spoken about my grief over James's death at two youth camps now. At the last one, a song came on—the same song that played at the funeral. I cried so hard and tried to get out of the room because it hurt so much to hear that song. One of the leaders came after me and brought me back, and everyone huddled around and gave me a big group hug. It was the best feeling I've ever had and helped me realise that it was okay to cry and that I was loved.

James's death has been so hard to come to terms with because I looked upon him as second brother. We all adored him. He was the most kind-hearted person you could ever meet. The irony was that he was completely anti-violence.

I still miss him and know I will for a long time.

What should you do?

Don't think about revenge—it is the worst thing you could ever do at a time like that. So many stupid, irrational thoughts go through your head. At the time it can seem like the most sensible solution in the world, but it's not. Talk through what you are thinking and feeling with someone you trust, so that you can see it for what it is.

Spend time with friends who knew the person and talk about all the good memories and great times you shared.

Know that it's okay to cry. Crying helps you release pent-up feelings of loss, anger and pain as you come to terms with your grief.

The grieving process can take a while, so let yourself feel whatever you are feeling, and talk to your friends.

Jess

In profile: Murray

Age: 13

Hair colour: Blond

Eye colour: Hazel

Greatest personal moment: Anytime I am playing football

Dream yet to accomplish: Ski in Switzerland

Favourite colour: Red

Favourite place in the world: Football grounds, as that's where I'm happiest

Best tip: Try to achieve your goals.

Dream for my future: To have a good supportive family

POWER STATEMENT

You've got your bad side and you've got your good side. When you're living in your bad side, you're not going to do anything good with your life. When you're living in your good side, there is so much potential and you can accomplish anything you put your mind to.

Chapter 17

GRIEVING THE DEATH OF A PARENT

It feels like the most unnatural thing in the world; losing one or both parents. The security that holds your world together disappears. Grief swallows you whole. Your world tilts and you know in the pit of your stomach that nothing will ever be the same again. Everything changes and you struggle to keep up with it all and deal with your emotions at the same time.

Finding someone to listen

Unspeakable sadness and grief are all encompassing. And although the intensity fades with time, the reality is still the same.

If you're feeling overwhelmed, a bereavement counsellor can help you come to terms with the loss and put the pieces of your life back together again. They are there to help, support and listen while you find your place in the world once more.

Melinda

I WAS THE ONLY ONE HOME WHEN DAD SUICIDED

When my dad was growing up, he didn't get on with his parents and was very unhappy at home. So when he turned eighteen he moved out. Around this time, he started smoking pot to relax and, after a while, became psychologically dependent on it. Because of the pot, Dad developed bipolar. He married Mum and ten years later, I was born, the second child after my brother, Jim.

Dad was the 'stay at home mum' and raised me and Jim while Mum went to work. We were very close and he was the centre of my world.

He decided to come off pot because he loved us so much. He said he didn't need it anymore because he had us.

Jim went to school two years ahead of me, and when I started school, Dad couldn't cope.

I was six years old when he committed suicide. My brother and mother were out, and he sent me to bed. I peeked out the window and saw him walking up the hill on our farm. That was the second last time I ever saw him. The last time, he was in a coffin.

I felt so much guilt over his death because I was the only one at home at the time. I wondered if there was something

I could have said or done that would have stopped him committing suicide.

I had trouble coming to terms with the fact that he knowingly took his own life and left me and Jim alone in the world without a father. I was sad, lonely and grieving.

The time that followed was a sad one for our family. My brother didn't talk about it at all. Although we'd always been close, he kept his distance most of the time.

My mum lost it for a while. She drank a lot, and gave us alcohol too. I don't think she coped at all. Suddenly she had to be two parents instead of one.

As time passed and we learned to deal with our grief, and home became comfortable again. We are closer as a family because we spent more time with Mum, which didn't happen until Dad's death because she was always working.

Jasmin

I LOST MY DAD AND MY GODSISTER DAYS APART

I loved my dad. Around the age of twelve, I felt as though everything was amazing in my life. I was living with Dad, my grades at school were excellent, I had a lovely boyfriend and I felt truly happy.

Then Dad became very sick. One day I came home and found him dead. I was shocked, I tried to wake him up, but I became desperate so called an ambulance. They couldn't revive him. When my brother arrived, I couldn't stop screaming. I felt distraught.

I had been Daddy's girl. And I missed him so much, more than words could say. His death left me feeling hollow.

The day after Dad died, my mother went away with her fiancé on their honeymoon. They weren't planning to marry for another few weeks, but wanted to do their honeymoon first so she could meet his family before the wedding.

The next day, I was faced with the news that my beloved godsister had been bitten by a snake and died. She was ten years old. I felt so guilty that she was younger than me. Her funeral was before Dad's. The sense of loss was overwhelming. I was about to turn thirteen and I'd experienced the deaths of two significant people in my life within days of each other.

After losing my dad and my godsister, I ached inside. I wanted a temporary solution, a distraction. I needed my mother to give me some love and attention—the nurturing kind of attention. But instead my mother emotionally and physically abused me.

So I started binge-drinking and partying to fill the void. I was trying to escape feelings I didn't want to face—because I felt so alone, with hardly any self-esteem, and I didn't have a strong parental role model, I had no-one to guide me.

Natashia

DAD'S DEATH LEFT ME FEELING ALL ALONE

My father died when I was ten. I was a happy kid, a tomboy who was as rough as guts, and I could take on anything. But behind closed doors I was a time bomb ready to explode. My father was my role model, the only one I would listen to. With him I couldn't get away with anything I did wrong, and that's what I needed. When he died I felt as if I was lost. My stepmother had taken my brother and sister away four years before to another country. My other brother was living with his mum, and my mother had issues of her own. I felt alone.

My grandma would always ask what was wrong. I never spoke about my dad's death because I didn't want to upset anyone. I didn't know how to deal with it, so I did what everyone else did and tried to ignore it.

And then I lost Mum too . . .

I was excited to finish school and start work. But Mum had me worried as she wasn't herself. I thought maybe she's just changing and coming to terms with the fact that I was growing up. She knew I was smoking pot and doing pills, but she never brought it up. I think she didn't want to fight.

My mum became really sick with a viral infection, which led to gangrene in her big toe. I took her to the hospital on Christmas Eve and they promised that she'd be fine. I'll never forget the look in my mother's eyes.

I looked up to her all these years as this powerful, strong, bubbly, assertive, person. She was my idol and she was scared, I was scared. I didn't know what to say or what to do.

I'd been out shopping for her Christmas present and when I rang her I knew something was wrong. She was crying and said, 'I need you to meet me at the hospital.' My heart sank. I jumped in a cab and was there in ten minutes. Not knowing what to expect, I cried all the way. I went to find her and that's when I saw my mother at her weakest—she looked pale and so tired. I gave her a kiss and asked what was wrong. She turned to me and said, 'I don't want to lose my toe, I don't want to be sick anymore.'

Mum told me she didn't want to die

Walking into the emergency department, pushing my mum in a wheelchair, I promised myself I wouldn't cry. Doctors came and inspected her toe and the lack of blood flowing to her legs. I saw how scared she was. She turned to me and said, 'I don't want to die.' I held her hand and reassured her she wouldn't. After eight doctors and a series of tests, she was released with antibiotics. She was still in pain so I took her to my grandmother's so we were close to the hospital.

That Christmas Eve was one of the worst days in my life. I washed my mother's swollen body, and watched her go through agonising pain. Christmas Day wasn't any better. My stepdad arrived at my grandmother's drunk and abusive and he got into an argument with Mum. I got mad at her for putting up with it so I refused to talk to her and we had a fight. Besides the arguments we attempted to have a good day. I had to go to work and Mum stayed over at Nan's for three days. I called to see if she was okay; she sounded happy but still in pain.

She's gone

The following Monday I was at work and due for a break. I left my phone on my desk, and when I returned there were two missed calls from my stepdad and a voicemail. This was unusual. I ran to the bathroom and called him. 'She's gone,' he said.

My heart felt like it was torn out of my chest. I kept saying in my head, this is a dream, it's not real, she's going to be fine.

I got to the hospital and ran to the front desk and frantically asked for my mother. I ran up two flights of stairs and then everything became slow. I saw bed 24 with the nurse laying fresh sheets and my heart sped up. 'Where's my mum, she's supposed to be here?'

The nurse took me to the Counsellor's Room where my stepdad, stepbrother and grandparents all stood in silence. A man came over and told me I'd better sit down. I sat next to my stepdad, his face streaming with tears. The man said, 'I'm sorry, your mum is dead.'

I wanted to see her one last time. I touched her face. I kept saying, 'She's so cold, get her a blanket, she's cold.' I held her hand, kissed her. 'Mum wake up, Mum wake up, come on Mum wake up, you can't do this Mum.' I fell backwards onto the floor, my head in my hands. My world stopped. I was broken.

I couldn't think, I was just blank, speechless, lost. At home I looked in the mirror, and touched my face. 'She's gone,' I whispered to myself. I stayed the night at a close friend's house, but I couldn't sleep. I was scared.

I fell deep into depression, even though I was trying hard to be strong. I waited for my aunty and uncle to come up from interstate and felt relieved when my whole family was together. For once I had a real family, but I wished Mum was there to be with me.

We organised the funeral, a white casket, colourful and beautiful gerberas, and my mother's life anthem 'Oh Life'.

The day of the funeral, I felt empty. I cried a river that day. My speech read, 'The day I lost my dad, I lost my heart, the day I lost my mother, I lost my spirit and my love for life.

The first time she heard me sing, she cried, so I'm singing this song for her.' I sang 'No-One' by Alicia Keys, a song that made my mum so proud, a song I dedicated to her. I loved her so much.

Looking back

Sometimes I lie awake, and think of my dreams as well as the battles I've had and the issues I've faced and have conquered. And every time someone says, 'You're just like your mum', I feel proud. I miss her more each day. Now that both my parents are gone, I realise I am alone. The only people I have now are my aunty and uncle, my brother and grandmother. They are my rocks; I never knew I had such support until I lost Mum.

Veronica

BOTH MY DADS COMMITTED SUICIDE

My dad suicided when I was three years old. I don't really remember him, but when I was old enough to understand what had actually happened, it hurt to realise that he left us intentionally and that he didn't want to know me.

My mum remarried a year later and I tried to get close to my stepdad but he and Mum were drunk all the time. He also used heroin frequently. Often he would verbally and physically abuse me, my two brothers and my sister. Mum never intervened when this was going on and it hurt that she didn't stand up for us.

I felt as though no-one cared about me.

On several occasions, we were taken away and placed in care. We spent several years being moved around between home, my aunty's place and my nan's place.

When I was eleven, my stepfather suicided. He overdosed on heroin. This happened after my brothers and sister and I were taken away from him because of his drug abuse. He left a suicide note and all it said was, 'Life isn't worth living now. You can all go f**k yourselves.'

I was only just coming to terms with my father's suicide when that happened. I felt unspeakable grief and pain. I thought that life was cruel and had ripped me off and I didn't care about anything anymore.

Mum started smoking pot as well as getting drunk, so wasn't there for me in the way that I needed her to be. I started getting into fights at school and breaking into houses. I was out of control, stealing and hanging around with the wrong crowd.

When the police got involved, things became serious. I got to a point where I realised that the way I was choosing to deal with my grief wasn't healthy. I knew if I didn't change the path I was on, I'd end up on the run or in gaol. I only really realised this after bonding with other people who had lost people they love. For the first time I talked about how I felt, how much pain I was in, and the guilt and shame that I was bottling up. People listened to me; they understood because they had been there and come through the other side. It was the first time I could see my situation for exactly what it was, and I was filled with a desperate need to change my life, to transform my horrible experience and turn it into something positive.

How I turned this around

I'm training to be a youth leader so I can help other teenagers who have lost a parent to suicide.

Trust that there is a way through

Listen to other people who have coped with grief, and what they did to get through it. Hearing how others coped is what helped me face my grief and this is what allowed me to work through it. And practise forgiveness. Even though my mum smokes pot and drinks all the time, I always say to her, 'Mum, I love you for who you are, not what you do'.

Murray

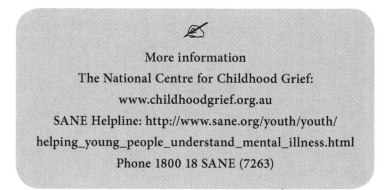

More information
The National Centre for Childhood Grief:
www.childhoodgrief.org.au
SANE Helpline: http://www.sane.org/youth/youth/
helping_young_people_understand_mental_illness.html
Phone 1800 18 SANE (7263)

An expert's view

The death of a friend or someone in your own age group can be confronting. The natural fear is, *If it can happen to them, it can happen to me*. It upsets the natural order of things and you lose that feeling of safety. You may question the purpose of life—Who am I, where do I fit in and how am I valued? When this happens it challenges your previously held assumptions about life and the perception that death is a long way off and only old people die.

> ## Tip
> Grief makes you feel out of control because the grief is controlling you. It helps to surround yourself with friends and family who can do things beside you, such as driving you around, cooking and managing day-to-day chores, until you gain that sense of control again.

THE FIRST FOUR WEEKS

During the first four weeks, the body produces natural chemicals to help you cope with pain. This wears off between 4–8 weeks. Around this time, the people helping and caring for you will return to their own lives and this can create another feeling of loss.

What you'll need during the first four weeks:

- loving care from friends and family
- people to do things beside you
- soft foods that soothe and are easily digested, such as soup, yogurt, cereals, soft fruits and vegetables.

COMING TO TERMS WITH GRIEF

Grief is unfamiliar and therefore frightening. To feel panic is
not unusual. If others make our environment safe and help
us do what we need to do, then little by little the intensity
decreases until we get to a point where the space between
intense surges of grief increases. Sometimes when that happens
we start to panic that we are losing the connection with the
person who has died. When the pain is there all the time we
feel connected, as though they are close to us. Because of this
panic it is common to do something unconsciously that allows
the person to come into the foreground again to reassure us
they are still part of who we are. For example, tidying up their
things, touching their clothing, getting out photos or watching
a movie you saw together. This allows you to feel the strong
emotion of grief so that you feel close to the person.

Grief isn't something you get over, it's something you
learn to live with. Initially grief is in the foreground and is
all-consuming. Eventually grief moves to the background
and the intensity diminishes. However, sometimes one of our
senses will be stimulated and this can bring on feelings of
grief again. Unexpected circumstances can trigger this, such
as thinking we see the person in the street or in a crowd, or

just being in a crowd and feeling panic, smelling a perfume that reminds us of the person we love, or perhaps hearing special music.

When we grieve, we become an exaggerated version of who we are. For example, if a person tends to withdraw, they will become more withdrawn. Someone who is a doer will become more active. If you're a writer, you'll write more. To find clues to managing the pain, think about how you have managed stress in the past in a constructive manner (as opposed to destructive). How could you use this now to help you manage grief?

Tip

Building a new life around the empty space inside you will help you learn to live with the pain and emptiness. It will also help you learn that all emotions can co-exist—one doesn't have to cancel out the other. For example, we can be sad *and* happy at the same time.

BEREAVEMENT COUNSELLING

Not everybody needs or wants counselling—most of us just need to know it's available. If you are worried about yourself, or others are worried about you, if you are doing something that is potentially harmful to yourself or others, or you just want a grief check-up to see if there is anything else that might help, then counselling can be a good option, especially if the death of the person you love was sudden and traumatic.

In these situations, because the manner of death (accident, murder or suicide) is in the foreground, it is normal to experience imaginings of horrible scenarios which are overwhelming. A bereavement counsellor can help you replace those images and sensory responses so that you are able to take the manner of death to the background.

The counselling process also helps young people and children become comfortable with saying a word associated with the death, such as suicide, so the word loses power and is no longer terrifying. Through doing this, use of words such as 'suicide' or 'murder' outside a young person's safe environment can't cause them harm and the manner of death stops controlling them. It also brings the person who has died into the foreground so that you can reconnect with them as you build a new life.

GOING FORWARD

It's important to find individual ways of retaining a connection and honouring that person's life. What are the things you valued about that person? What do you miss the most? What parts of them do you want to take with you for the rest of your life?

BALANCING ACT

Mental health is maintained when we have a balance between our internal and external worlds. The internal is about our thought processes and emotions, the external is doing things, or having things done to or for us, all the things that impact on us from the outside. We learn a rhythm between the two as a result of our personality and the behaviours modelled for us in our families when we're growing up. When grieving, this rhythm is disrupted and the internal world becomes enormous, whereas the external world doesn't matter as much because we are consumed by the enormity of the emotion.

The relationship you had with the person who has died will always be a part of who you are. The struggle is in moving from the external tangible relationship where you can hold them and talk to them, to an internal experience—remembering sensory contact and enhancing memories with all the senses so you feel like you are still close to that person.

For young people, grief makes their internal world so huge—boring lessons in a classroom can't compete so they tend to daydream and underachieve. Some overachieve, trying to prove to themselves that they can survive.

It takes a while to restore the balance between the internal and external worlds. Distraction can help after the first four weeks to help you stop focusing on the loss every minute of every day. No-one can keep doing that forever.

Listen to your body and do what it tells you. Don't question it, trust your own instincts. Work out how long is a 'me' time to focus on what's happened, think about that person and enjoy memories of shared times, feel sadness, happiness or whatever emotions are close to the surface at the time, and think about when you need to be distracted with some other activity that previously would have been enjoyable.

You can't wait when you're grieving to *want* to do something. Instead, make a decision to do something and just do it. It's important not to expect pleasure. The most you can hope for is a sense of relief and an easing of tension.

Ultimately the balance between the external and internal will return and you will start to experience feelings of joy again. In the meantime, be kind to yourself. Grief is unpredictable and sometimes all you can do is lie on your back and float with the current.

Dianne McKissock OAM

Co Clinical Director, Bereavement Care Centre and National Centre for Childhood Grief

In profile: Jessica

Age: 16

Hair colour: Light and slightly dark brown

Eye colour: Blue

Favourite saying: 'So what?'

Greatest personal moment: Anytime I complete a big task

Dream yet to accomplish: Write a book

Favourite colour: Velvet red

Favourite place in the world: Anywhere there is no judgement

Best tip: Don't sit there, get up and do something about it.

Favourite quote: 'Happiness can be found even in the darkest of times if only one remembers to turn on the light.' *Harry Potter*

Dream for my future: To become a child protection worker, author and band member

POWER STATEMENT

Don't just let something happen; do something about it.

Have you heard of . . .
Inspire Foundation
www.inspire.org.au

Our dream is for a world where every young person can stand up and say 'I am happy'.

We combine technology with the direct involvement of young people to deliver innovative and practical online programs that prevent youth suicide and improve mental health and wellbeing.

Because the internet is accessible, anonymous, engaging and informative, and provides a space where you can feel empowered and confident to talk about sensitive issues, that is where Inspire is.

Our programs include Reach Out and ActNow.

Reach Out—www.reachout.com.au—can help you work out who to talk to and where to find help in the community, or how to assist a friend in need. Reach Out also offers information, support and resources to help you improve your understanding of mental health issues, develop resilience, and increase coping skills and help-seeking behaviour.

ActNow—www.actnow.com.au—can help you feel more connected to each other and the community, and feel as though you have a voice and can make a difference—factors known to have an impact on mental health and wellbeing. We strive always to keep our hearts warm and our heads cool, because that way we will help more people lead happier lives.

What is Inspire's personal message to young people facing hardship?

- You are not alone and there are services, and people, who care and want to help very much.
- We strongly believe in the strength, focus and abilities of all young people and Inspire helps to provide them with the tools, connections, community and information that they need to lead a happier life.

Charlotte Beaumont-Field
Wellbeing Manager, Inspire Foundation

Finding a way through

Just when I thought my life could not get any more complicated, throughout my high school years I found myself trying to support three of my closest friends who were suicidal to the point where they were self-harming.

One of them made a comment that stayed with me to this day: 'If you tell anyone about what I tell you, you will regret it, I won't just attempt to kill myself, I will actually do it.'

At that point I felt that I couldn't seek help from anyone—not people in the community, not phone counselling services—at the risk of losing a friend who I considered a sister.

So I turned to the internet for help, hoping that I could find some information to tell me what I should do.

Soon I came across the Reach Out website and I could not believe what I had found. This was exactly what I was after: easy to navigate, a range of fact sheets on issues and information on where to find help.

Finding this website has changed my life and may have even saved my life. I told my friends about the Reach Out website and thankfully got a positive response from them. They told me that they found the information very useful in working out what was going on in their lives. For me personally I cannot express in words how much the Reach Out website impacted my life. For the first time I started to understand what I was going through, had strategies to help myself get through my tough time, and knew where I could find the help that I needed.

Daniel

Inspire's dream for young people

Our dream is that every young person
Can stand up and say:
I am a young person.
I am loved and I love.
There lies before me a land of endless
opportunity where I can learn and grow.
There lies within me a limitless ocean of
compassion and kindness.
I respect all people, including myself,
for who we are.

I celebrate our common humanity and
I honour our individual differences.
I show up for life each morning ready for
whatever comes my way.
I give my best and know it will make
all the difference.
I am making the world a better place.
I am happy.

Inspire Foundation

Chapter 18

THERE IS ALWAYS A TURNING POINT

'Happiness is like a butterfly which, when pursued, is always beyond our grasp, but, if you will sit down quietly, may alight upon you.'

Nathaniel Hawthorne

When you come through a traumatic period and find a sense of peace, it is natural to fear something else may happen to rob you of contentment. But life will throw stuff at you and that's just life. Once you have found that sense of peace, it will always be there. The trick is tapping into it. If you don't like how life is feeling right now, go inside yourself and find that peaceful place. If you have trouble quieting your mind, visualise your ideal holiday spot, or a place with special memories, and picture yourself there. What does it look like? What can you hear/smell/taste?

In this place, nothing holds any power over you.

Life is a balancing act

There are different degrees of suffering. Life is about juggling things until you get to a place of acceptance. Try to look at problems as challenges and think about what you can learn from them. When it comes to how you are going to deal with something, there is always a choice—and how you react to a problem is the only thing you can control.

Melinda

'It's choice—not chance—that determines your destiny.'
Jean Nidetch

OVERDOSING WAS MY WAKE-UP CALL

As a result of being sexually abused at age ten, I became consumed by depression, and slipped into destructive behaviours including self-harm and bulimia. My turning point came after I tried, unsuccessfully, to overdose on Panadol. I had to have my liver checked for residual damage and this frightened me to the point where I was shaking, terrified that I had done permanent damage to my liver.

The test was normal but it was the wake-up call I needed.

I decided that the person who abused me had already taken away most of my teenage years, and I didn't want to give him the satisfaction of ruining my life. I wanted to become stronger, change my ways, become a survivor.

As I learned to cope with my depression, and deal with self-harm, the episodes of bulimia became less. I found that my destructive behaviours didn't give me that same level of release anymore because I'd started turning towards more positive things. Instead of sitting around moping, I became involved in life and started to embrace it.

Now if I'm feeling down, I will talk to someone about it, which in turn helps me talk myself out of it. Then I choose to take positive action, such as an activity that brings me joy, instead of a negative or destructive one.

If you're feeling lost . . .

- Talk to someone you trust. There is always help out there, you just have to go and find it.
- Help yourself first and foremost—you have the strength to pull through, you just have to find it within yourself. People can be there for you, but in the end you need to be the one to help yourself.
- Even in your darkest moment remember there is a light at the end of the tunnel. As clichéd as that sounds—and I admit I didn't believe anyone who told me that when I was going through the hard times I faced—it's very true.
- Find a creative outlet that is helpful and positive, such as writing or painting. I wrote a lot of poems, and I also used these to show people how I was feeling and so people could understand what I was going through.

I believe I've been through quite a bit throughout the small amount of life I've had, but I wouldn't change it because it's made me who I am today. It's opened my eyes and shown me life is worth everything. It's matured me and made me so much stronger to deal with anything else that comes my way.

Lauren

I FOUND PEOPLE WITH STRENGTH

By the beginning of Year 12, my abusive stepfather finally left for good. I also changed my group of friends so I was no longer surrounded by negative influences. I became a better judge of who I chose to keep company with. I started to do well again at school. I even stayed after school, studying late into the night. I met another guy who had a similar family background, and we used to stay back at school and study together. We soon became close friends. I also became friends with a girl who had a good, stable family and I spent a lot of time at her place. We ended up dating for seven or eight years. Being around strong and stable people was a major influence in how I began to feel on the inside, and the way in which I viewed the world and my place in it started to change.

During the tough times, I let myself feel the pain. I didn't block it out, so I was able to deal with it. I think expressing my feelings helped me get past them and move on, instead of dwelling on the past and allowing it to continuously affect me.

Tom

MY BEST FRIEND'S SUICIDE SCARED ME

I saw myself going down the same path and I didn't want to die. I gave up alcohol and went back home. But my stepfather continued to abuse me. Because of all I'd been through, I decided I wasn't going to take it anymore. I became so angry that I retaliated violently towards him. This was my way of standing up to him and showing him that I wasn't going to put up with his abuse any longer.

After that I moved across the state to stay with my dad. It was a better environment, but I still couldn't bring myself to tell anyone about my best friend's death and I became really quiet. The only way I could deal with the pain was to sleep all day and keep my feelings and emotions bottled up.

A few months later, my sister told me about Youth Insearch camps. The first few camps I kept to myself because I felt suicidal, but the fourth one there was a session about friends and I ended up breaking down and talking about my best friend.

This was the first time that people listened to what I was saying. I wasn't used to having anyone listen to me and for once I felt loved and accepted. That experience was a true turning point for me. I realised that I was able to talk about whatever I felt I needed to as long as I felt safe.

I'm still living with my dad and, although we hit some rough spots every now and again, things are going well and I've never been happier.

I'm more open now and starting to think more positively about myself and my future.

Justin

ONLY I COULD HELP MYSELF

Between the ages of thirteen and sixteen, I was out of control. I felt angry at everyone and the world. I had the normal adolescent angst but that coupled with all my other issues made me feel alone in the world. No-one listened to me. No-one believed me.

As I got older and better at self-injuring, most of my cuts needed stitches. I'd take myself to the doctor and they'd want to know how I did it. I was honest and made sure people in the local hospital knew me. I've had bad experiences with GPs. One refused to give me a local anaesthetic. He said if I liked pain, he was going to give me what I wanted and stitched me up without any anaesthetic. He was horrible. I ended up telling Mum about it and she made a passionate complaint. But I'm still angry at her for not believing me about Dad sexually abusing me. (I'm 22 now and Mum still doesn't believe me.)

My turning point came when I was sixteen. With maturity, I started to realise I had to help myself. No-one else was going to help me.

I searched for information on self-injury but couldn't find much. I wanted to know what it was all about, and strategies to overcome it. I decided to create a pamphlet on self-injury with a local youth service, but it never got distributed because there was no money to do it.

After my move interstate, I brought it to my counsellor's attention, and told her I wanted to get the pamphlet off the ground to help other young people who are self-injuring. My counsellor was able to source funding and the pamphlet was distributed. I was so happy!

I now work closely with a community service that has a specialised project on self-injury, and I'm an advocate for people who don't have anyone to talk to. I speak at conferences about my experiences in care as well as self-injury, because for me the two are closely linked.

If I had my teenage years over again, I wouldn't change anything, even though it was so hard at times that I believed I'd be better off dead. I don't know who I'd be without any of this. I'm now motivated to help people because of the trauma I've suffered.

Amy

MY TURNING POINT CAME WHEN MUM REACHED OUT TO ME

It felt so good to be listened to, to know that my feelings did matter, and that I wasn't alone.

The psychologist helped me by teaching me techniques and skills to better deal with things.

I learned how to practise mindfulness. When walking to school, I'd concentrate on placing one foot in front of the other and looking at things around me, so I was fully present in the moment.

Now if I'm having bad day, I ask myself what I can do to make it better, and what I can do to feel better about myself. One thing I learned was to compile a list of the things I love to do that bring me happiness. These include listening to my favourite music, going shopping with friends and seeing a funny movie. I also learned how to set goals and create a plan to work towards them to make them a reality.

Abby

I GOT TO THE POINT WHERE I REALISED 'THIS ISN'T WHO I AM'

I'd always been a good girl, a straight-A student, and all of a sudden my life had drastically gone downhill.

I thought, *This is not who I am destined to be.*

I realised I had to put the effort in, and I was the only one who could save myself.

Natashia

I DECIDED I NEEDED HELP

When my brother moved here from another country, going on walks became our therapeutic sessions. We sat at the park with no words spoken, then he looked to me with tears in his eyes and said, 'I look up to you, please don't leave me, you're the only family I've got. I don't like to see you this upset.' It was right then I realised I wasn't only hurting myself, I was hurting my brother. It was at that point I decided I needed help. And in between work and school, I started to study and read books. Instead of getting letters sent home from school about afternoon detentions, I stayed back at the library and studied, determined to turn my life around.

Veronica

I REALISED I WAS LIVING IN DENIAL

I self-harmed on my wrists one day. This was a cry for help. I was screaming on the inside, struggling to understand what was wrong with me and why my mother didn't love me.

My best friend at school saw the scars and promised she wouldn't tell anyone. Then a teacher who I trusted confronted me and asked me what was wrong and I started crying. As I went to turn away, she grabbed my wrist to pull me back and it hurt so much. When she saw my reaction, she was concerned she may have hurt me so she pushed up my sleeve and then saw what I'd done. I knew she was obliged to report it.

As a result, I was sent to see a youth liaison officer. She was so kind and told me that I shouldn't feel as though I had to do everything I was doing at home with the babies. But I told her that I did it because I loved my family, and that was my way of showing that I loved them.

As I got to know and trust my youth liaison officer, I opened up to her about a lot of things that were troubling me, including (eventually) my self-harm. She pointed out that self-harming was not showing that I loved myself. This made me think really hard about why I wanted to harm myself.

The thing that broke me was when I realised I was being as fake as my mother. I was sinking to her level so I could feel I had a connection with her.

At the same time I realised that my friends all had such lovely mums, and I wondered why I couldn't have a lovely mum too.

When my sister was four she said to me, 'We don't have a mum like everyone else's mum.' The fact that even she knew this at such a young age made me realise how much was missing in my life, and how badly I was in denial.

Bronte

> I learned that I am not alone, there are people worse off than me, and that I don't need drugs or alcohol to be happy. I'm a hard worker if I put my mind to something. I have learned to love myself and accept myself for who I am.
>
> Meg

FORGING NEW FRIENDSHIPS CHANGED MY WORLD

The toughest moments were before I went to live with my aunty. I felt desperately unhappy and guilty for the pain I'd caused Mum. I turned to drugs and alcohol to try and hide the pain. At home I'd pick fights with everyone because I couldn't have any drugs or alcohol there. What really helped was listening to certain music that suited my mood and staying in my room, away from everyone.

The police referred me to Youth Insearch and I went on my first camp. It was the first time in a long time I felt accepted and loved for who I am. I made friends easily and felt happy for the first time in ages.

My aunty was heavily into drugs and she was always fighting with my uncle and nan. We hardly had any food in the fridge—I realised that my life wasn't so bad when I was with Mum. So I worked hard to try and convince Mum to let me come home.

The youth camp and support I received from there helped me change my attitude towards others and my behaviour at school. All I wanted was to get my life back on track and to be back with my family.

Meg

I LEARNED TO LISTEN TO MYSELF

Eventually I found a support worker who helped me deal with Dad's death and my mother's addiction, as well as anger management.

Now, if I feel anger starting to build, I go into my sister's room and talk it out. This helps me cope with the things I can't control. Being listened to, loved and nurtured by my sister is a wonderful feeling. She helps me stay calm. The other thing I do is go outside and surround myself with nature. I love gardening and this has proven to be a healthy distraction. If anger blindsides me, I go outside and punch the ground, and stay outside until the feelings subside.

Unfortunately, I've had to accept that my mother may never change. AA can't help her because she won't admit she has a drinking problem. We even tried intervention but my mother denies she has a problem and says she needs to manage it on her own. We know she can't. Until she gets to the point where she wants to help herself, it will always be going on in the background. But I'm learning to manage it and that's all I can do.

Daniel

FINDING THE RIGHT COUNSELLOR

I knew I had to do something to change my life. I was sad and miserable all the time and couldn't seem to find happiness in anything I did.

I started seeing a counsellor and things have slowly improved. It's so important to find someone you connect with. I've been through a string of counsellors trying to find the right one for me, and while some have been okay, I'm still searching for one I feel I can trust implicitly, who will be able to help me the way I need to be helped. I'll know them when I find them.

Jasmin

SHARING MY LIFE WITH SOMEONE SPECIAL

I went out with a guy who made me feel really good about myself. He showed me how to look at the brighter side of things and made me feel as though I was worthy of love. It was a wonderful feeling. We eventually broke up, but we're still very close.

Jess

An Expert's View

Q: I'M FEELING LOST AND ALONE AND TOO SCARED TO SEEK HELP. WHAT SHOULD I DO?

A: If you are scared to seek help or have no idea where to start, you should check out services like Reach Out at www.reachout.com.au. You will be able to access many fact sheets about a range of issues and the good thing is that you can do this without anyone knowing. You might be embarrassed or scared to ask someone about an issue face-to-face or over the phone, so Reach Out provides a way for you to find the information you need without having to work up the courage to ask someone.

There are also stories written by teens who have gone through some really tough times. If you read these stories, you can see how they've worked through these times and can take some tips and ideas from them.

The ROtreat forums are a place where you can learn new skills and ways to handle tricky issues, as well as providing a place to hang out, run groups and have special guest speakers who discuss a range of topics that you may need help with. The best thing about the forums is that you can remain anonymous and the RO Crew + RO Community are there to make sure the forums stay safe.

Charlotte Beaumont-Field

Wellbeing Manager, Inspire Foundation

At Kids Helpline each and every caller is treated as a unique individual with their own particular balance of problems and strengths. When a young person contacts us, a counsellor will take the time to listen to what is happening for them in their life, build a personal connection, and then begin to explore with the young person different perspectives and ideas that they may find useful in beginning to deal with their issues. The counselling relationship is most useful when new ideas are jointly developed between the counsellor and the caller.

If you are feeling lost and alone, take a chance and reach out to Kids Helpline. Sharing your concerns with a counsellor may be a bit scary at first, but we have eighteen years of feedback to say that sharing concerns this way has been very helpful to thousands of young people. Call 1800 55 1800.

Wendy Protheroe

General Manager Counselling Services, Kids Helpline

Chapter 19

YES, YOU CAN CHANGE PERSPECTIVE

'All the world is full of suffering. It is also full of overcoming.'
Helen Keller

Life is precious and it is up to *you* to create your own experience. If you find yourself caught up in a cycle of persistent negative thoughts, your experience of life is going to be largely negative. The more you focus on the positive aspects of your world, and live with a sense of trust and excitement about what the future holds, you will naturally create a happier and more meaningful experience.

Change your mental attitude

Negative thought processes lead to self-doubt, which in turn erodes self-esteem. If you learn to turn your way of thinking around by replacing negative thoughts with positive thoughts, you will begin to develop a more positive outlook.

- Catch negative thoughts as they occur
  - Becoming aware of your thoughts is a constant conscious effort at first. What you think will create what you feel, so as soon as you start to feel your mood declining, consciously pause your thoughts. Back-track your thoughts until you reach the one that triggered a negative response. Then reframe the thought so it has a positive spin.
  - In every situation there is a choice. Choose to think positive thoughts instead of discouraging ones.
  - Write a list of things in your life that you are grateful for.
  - Write a list of things about yourself that you love.
  - When you catch a negative thought process, choose one thing from each list and think about how grateful you are for these things, how wonderful they make you feel, and how your life is so much richer because of them.

- Read inspirational material
  - From affirmation cards, to your favourite self-awareness books, keep these close and refer to them at random during the day.

- Think about others
  - Make an extra effort to help other people. Be kind and thoughtful about the needs of others. It is a known fact that random acts of kindness elevate your mood.

Helping other people is gratifying. It also teaches you about healthy relationships.

- Take care of your personal needs
  - Maintaining a positive mindset comes more easily if you're looking after yourself. Make sure you have a good sleep pattern as well as a healthy balance of food and exercise.
  - As you close your eyes to go to sleep, visualise your favourite place in the world and let your imagination play out a scene. This will help you relax and will promote feelings of contentment and happiness.

- Learn contentment
  - Think about what you have in your world that makes you happy, and the brilliant future waiting for you. Live in the present and be grateful for all your blessings.
  - When going through periods of heartache or difficulty, remember that in a crisis we are more focused. Adversity allows us to learn more about ourselves and grow as human beings. These experiences also mean that you will be able to help others going through something similar, and therefore turn the experience into a positive.

Melinda

'Change your thoughts and change your world.'

Norman Vincent Peale

When negative feelings strike

Of course there will be times something awful happens and you feel yourself sinking. During these times, give yourself permission to feel. Acknowledge the emotion whether it's fear, sadness, anger or grief, and surrender to the feelings. This will help the feelings to pass sooner because you are not resisting, you are allowing them to be.

Go somewhere quiet and spend some time reflecting. Sometimes we need to process an event or situation before we can make sense of it.

Eventually these feelings will pass and when they do, you will have greater clarity and purpose.

Melinda

'Self-pity is our worst enemy and if we yield to it, we can never do anything good in the world.'

Helen Keller

CHANGING YOUR PERSPECTIVE

My first ever reference was written by my Year 9 coordinator: 'Tom has the enviable quality of being able to look at any point of conflict from many perspectives.'

To me, perspective means this: All our experiences have the potential to cause us to grow or to sink. It all comes down to how we see it and how we respond to it; what perspective we choose to take on.

The idea promoted by popular culture is that if a particular thing 'happens' to you, it will cause you to feel a particular way. A culture of blame ensues, and legitimate as it may seem, it disempowers people because it puts the source and cause of all their life's problems outside of them.

The idea of responsibility is grounded in the belief that between stimulus and response, we have a choice. That is, when something 'happens', we can respond in ways that we choose. This isn't saying that it's not okay to feel down if something happens that is not to our liking. It's okay to feel upset by something, and it's okay to feel sad. The important thing is to realise that on some level we're choosing that response, and when the time's right and with a new perspective on the event, we'll choose a different response.

Tom

LET PEOPLE IN

It's taken a long time for my confidence to grow, and it hasn't been easy. What helped me the most was reaching out and trusting others, and letting them in. Knowing that people cared enough about me to listen and want to help made me feel important.

I have more confidence now. I recently completed Year 10 and that gave me an enormous sense of achievement, which was great for my self-esteem.

I've always wanted to help people, and to see people happy not sad. I know what it's like to be sad, and I'd rather people experience happiness and joy because they are more fulfilling emotions.

Emma

Chapter 20

COPING STRATEGIES FOR EVERYDAY LIFE

'The only things that stand between a person and what they want in life are the will to try it, and the faith to believe it's possible.'

Rich Devos

If everything is getting you down and you feel 'stuck', remember that making positive changes in your life will lead you to somewhere you once hoped or imagined you'd be. Taking a chance on something gives you the opportunity to see how it feels and whether you believe in it enough to want to pursue it.

Healing yourself

Alone time can be healing because it allows you to reflect on your situation or circumstance and process your feelings.

It also provides the chance to monitor your thoughts and become aware of your inner dialogue. Once you gain a sense of the nature of your thoughts and the way they influence your feelings and emotions, you have the ability to turn them into strong, positive ideals. Positive thoughts create happiness. You create your own experience by the way you choose to be. Stay focused on believing in yourself and all you can be, and open your heart to love and happiness.

Melinda

A decision-making exercise

If you are confused about a decision, try this.

Find a quiet spot where you won't be interrupted, lie down and close your eyes. Picture your life with one possible outcome and focus on how it might feel. Stay with this feeling for a while until you are really familiar with what it feels like. Then picture your life with the other outcome. What does it feel like now? Which scenario felt 'lighter'—that feeling of 'anything is possible' or 'happiness' or 'joyous'. Which scenario felt more like you were 'stuck'?

Whenever I have a fork in my road, this helps me decide which way to go—the one that feels lighter and happier is the one I choose, because this means I'm not restricting myself to an outcome that feels 'limited'.

Switching off logic and tuning into your feelings is when you instinctively know which decision feels right for you. It doesn't matter if it makes no sense. Trust your gut feeling and trust the future.

Melinda

MAKING PEACE WITH DAD'S DEATH

One of my goals was to scatter Dad's ashes. I used to suffer from recurring nightmares—sometimes Dad's death would play out before my eyes, other times he was angry, demanding that I put him at peace. These nightmares unnerved me and because I tried not to dwell on them, they became a block that disturbed my sleep. The breakthrough came when I decided to scatter Dad's ashes. It was nine years later, but it felt like the right time to do it. I was old enough to understand that he was in so much pain he thought we'd be better off without him. I stopped feeling guilty. And I wanted to honour Dad and, in a sense, set him free.

Picturing my dad at peace while listening to a recording of a meditation that focuses on feeling safe and happy has helped me so much. Now when I close my eyes, I picture my dad thanking me and there is a sense of peace around him.

It's important to have a goal, somewhere you want to go, or something you want to do, instead of wandering aimlessly through life. Setting goals means you are in tune with yourself and your hopes and dreams.

My goal now is to help others. I'm keen to explore social work so I can counsel other young people who have lost their way and need help to find their path.

Jasmin

'Your imagination is your preview of life's coming attractions.'

Albert Einstein

Here are some insights I'd like to share that I have learned along the way:

- It matters not what others think. It's how you feel about yourself that is important.
- Be true to yourself even if it means hurting someone's feelings.
- Let life surprise you.
- If something in your life is changing, embrace it. Change is part of the learning and growing process and allows you to discover positive aspects of yourself.
- Have faith in your instincts and trust yourself first and foremost.
- In times of uncertainty look into your heart; answers always come from within.
- In every moment, be the best you can be.
- Everyday there are opportunities all around. Be open to them and watch what unfolds.

Melinda

An expert's view

Q: WHAT IS THE BEST WAY TO BECOME MORE AWARE OF MY THOUGHTS AND MAKE SENSE OF MY FEELINGS?

A: Often our behaviours, thoughts and reactions are automatic—we do them unconsciously without being aware of them at all. Ever had your mother say, 'Stop biting your nails', and you had no idea how your hand even got to your mouth? Ever found yourself finishing off a whole packet of chips despite planning to leave half for another day? Or reacting to something a friend said and afterwards thinking, *Whoa, where did that come from?* because your reaction seemed too extreme?

By increasing self-awareness, which is defined as our insight into our thoughts, reactions and behaviours, we then have the power to choose and change those that are unhelpful. For example, by painting 'stop and grow' on your nails, you get a wake-up call whenever your hand drifts to your mouth. By slowing down the consumption of your packet of chips and 'consciously' savouring each bite with all your senses, you break the hand-to-mouth circuit and know when you are full. And by noticing the reaction rising within you when your friend says something hurtful, you can take the time to think before blurting a response you'll later regret.

SO, HOW DO YOU INCREASE
SELF-AWARENESS?

Different things work for different people but the following are beneficial for most:

Journalling

Getting your thoughts and feelings out on paper can be quite magical. It can either be stream of consciousness writing that is like a big mind-dump or you can structure it by highlighting what went well in the day, what didn't, how you felt, what you would do the same again and what you might do differently next time. Journal at the end of a day or just when you notice an uncomfortable feeling coming up within you. What is the feeling? What were you thinking beforehand? Was there a triggering event? Then you can usually look at what you might be able to do or think that is more helpful and may take some of the sting out of the feeling.

Finding a good sounding board

The reason it is called a 'sounding board' is because verbalising your thoughts and feelings to someone you trust helps get it off your chest and you also have them reflected back in a way that is much clearer. Be careful not to choose someone that will just want to tell you what to do though!

A problem shared is a problem halved

It depends who you share it with but, again, there is magic in getting it out, if not on paper, verbally to someone else— basically just out of your head. This helps un-jumble the confusion that can reign when it is all locked inside us. It might be a parent, friend, trusted relative, teacher or professional. There is always help out there—take responsibility for not carrying your burden alone.

Meditation, visualisation, relaxation, music and yoga

Anything in your busy world that allows time for stillness increases self-awareness. Deep breathing and focusing on each breath in and out for a ten-count, or working through each muscle group, tensing and then relaxing it, and then visualising a tranquil peaceful place with all of your senses helps create some stillness and 'white space'.

Exercise

For some, any form of sitting still is nearly impossible! In that case, a walking meditation, a jog or some high-impact aerobic exercise works well. Exercise burns energy and can shake off tension that keeps us locked in unhelpful thoughts and conversations in our head. It often also helps us feel better and gain a lighter perspective on problems.

Q: HOW CAN I LEARN TO UNDERSTAND MYSELF BETTER?

A: Once you have kept a diary or journalled for a while, you may start to notice recurring themes. You are becoming aware of the unconscious thoughts and assumptions you make. These are often based on the rules, values and beliefs you took on unconsciously when you were a young child and are influenced by your upbringing, the media, your culture and your circle of friends. Common ones are 'I must be liked by everyone', 'I need my parents' and friends' approval at all times', 'I must be thin and beautiful-looking to be worthwhile', 'Life should always be fair', 'I am not good enough', 'I am just a burden to my friends and family' . . . Any sound familiar?

Once you realise these 'rules', you can stop living your life by them if they no longer serve you or are unrealistic.

Tessa Marshall

Director, Marshall Coaching Group

In profile: Kerry

Age: 13

Hair colour: Brown/black

Eye colour: Brown

Favourite saying: 'Never say you can't.'

Greatest personal moment: Helping others during the Youth Insearch program

Dream yet to accomplish: Finish school and become a vet

Favourite colour: Purple

Favourite place in the world: The beach, because I don't live near one and love it when I can get to one

Best tip: Don't give up.

Dream for my future: Get into university so I can work towards my dream of becoming a vet

Chapter 21

HELPING SOMEONE YOU LOVE—FOR FRIENDS, PARENTS AND CARERS

'Kind words can be short and easy to speak, but their echoes are truly endless.'

Mother Teresa

In a world where there is conflict, confusion and a lack of emotional security, it is my personal belief that we need to empower the people we love to be true to what is in their hearts and provide them with coping mechanisms to foster trust and belief in themselves.

It can be difficult standing by and watching someone you love suffering. But there are ways to help:

- Be supportive and patient.
- Encourage the person you love to do the things that they enjoy.

- Give them hope in any way you can. Help them set goals and engage them in conversation about their dreams for the future.
- Let them know you love them no matter what.
- Help them find a counsellor or therapist.

Don't forget the importance of looking after yourself too. Emotions such as frustration, anger and fear may come up from time to time. It's important to develop a support system and a network of trusted friends so you have someone to vent your feelings to.

> I think it is really important that people who know someone facing a struggle continue to stand by them, support them, love them and help remind them of the good times and things to look forward to. Even if the person struggling turns you away, be sure to always come back because they don't want people giving up on them. Even if they want to be alone, they still need to know someone is there.
>
> **Abby**

The people we love need to not only *know* they are loved, but to *be shown* love in actions and deeds. A supportive and caring family environment is a safety net. Everyone needs to feel their family will buoy them through tough times, listen to their fears and celebrate their successes instead of pressuring them to do or be more. Friends are important too because they are trusted confidants and beacons of light.

Love is the key; to know that your family and friends love you and are proud of you means everything.

Melinda

Remember that young people are very good at supporting each other. Their peer group is important to them and this is a strength of the age group. What we do in the community, in terms of teaching meditation techniques and encouraging self-development, among other things, builds up skills in a positive manner and this can't help but have an impact on young people.

Vikki Ryall

Clinical Manager, headspace National Office

In profile: Simon

Age: 17

Hair colour: Blond

Eye colour: Greeny-blue

Greatest personal moment: Making a difference in anything I do

Dream yet to accomplish: Work for Qantas as an engineer

Favourite colour: Blue

Favourite place in the world: Fiji

Best tip: No matter what life throws at you, never give up.

Dream for my future: To have a family of my own

POWER STATEMENT

Never stop trying and always give your all and do your best. Even if you get something wrong you can learn from it and do better next time.

Chapter 22

IF YOU KNEW THEN WHAT YOU KNOW NOW

'Optimism is the faith that leads to achievement.
Nothing can be done without hope and confidence.'

Helen Keller

If I could go back and tap my 13-year-old self on the shoulder to unleash a few pearls of wisdom, one thing I would tell myself is this: ***Always be true to yourself.***

All too often we can get caught up in other people's opinions, worrying what others will think or how we'll be judged if we do something that goes against the norm. Other times we go along with things to fit in with someone else's expectations.

If you're always true to yourself, when something doesn't feel right you'll know instinctively that it isn't.

It can be scary to say out loud how you are feeling inside, but life is moment to moment, and unless we speak up for ourselves in the moment, that moment will pass. Never be stuck doing something you don't want to do just because someone else believes you should.

Sometimes being true to yourself means hurting someone's feelings. This is never pleasant, but self-respect and peer respect come when you act with integrity and honesty. Be genuine and respect other people's feelings—*say what you mean*, not what you think someone wants to hear.

Melinda

'Aerodynamically the bumblebee shouldn't be able to fly, but the bumblebee doesn't know that so it goes on flying anyway.'

Mary Kay Ash

If I could go back and tell myself something, I would tell myself to stay away from the friends I was hanging around and that I don't need the drugs or alcohol. I can be strong on my own, if I listen to myself.

Meg

If you find yourself in a bad place, talk to someone you trust.

Think of progress as a ladder—one step at a time. It can be a long process but you don't have to feel alone.

Vent your emotions by playing sport or going for a walk. Make sure you are active. Don't do what I did and sit in your room for days on end, as this will only make you feel even more hopeless.

Alexis

Signs you are not coping

If you find that you are taking everything to heart, you are not coping. Loss of confidence, worrying what everyone else thinks of you, antisocial behaviour and not wanting to go out or do anything are also signs. If any of these occur, step back and think about what's really going on. Talk it through with a trusted friend.

Alexis

After I was raped by my friend's boyfriend I learned to never bottle things up. One thing I wish I knew then was that I wasn't alone. For anyone else in that situation, it is *never* your fault. Talk to someone you trust and take a stand and represent the girls that may be too afraid to speak out. You have to stick together. It is my wish that one day we will have enough say in the world to reduce the incidence of sexual assault.

Natashia

The strategies that worked for me

Talking it out. When I started counselling I didn't talk at all, I'd just shrug my shoulders. Gradually I learned to trust, to open up, and that's when I felt the greatest sense of release and personal freedom.

Finding a distraction—writing, drawing and painting—were ways of self-expression and allowed me to vent my emotions. The theme for my major artwork for my HSC was sexual abuse and this helped me to let it go.

Lauren

Surround yourself with a support network of people you trust, admire and aspire to be. Who you are and who you become has a lot to do with the people you have in your life. I was fortunate I had male teachers who were strong positive role models.

Keep questioning things, and learn as much as you can by observing.

Look for new perspectives on things, and different ways of analysing experiences and situations.

Be open to feedback, as this can be a great opportunity to learn. Instead of taking it personally, choose to listen and learn something from it.

Language creates our world because language communicates meaning. Choose your words to exemplify what you really mean.

Learn to respect boundaries as they condense and define our experiences.

Define the direction you want to take and adopt a collaborative approach. If you work in with others, they will support you in return.

Tom

In times of hardship it's so important to keep your head up high and remember that good memories can save your life. Have faith that things will turn out for the best, and keep believing in yourself. Let no-one take you for granted; stand up for yourself and what you believe in and you will find your strength.

Justin

You are put on this earth to do something special. You can do anything your heart desires so don't waste your life being unhappy. Find help; learn how to make yourself happy and live life to the fullest.

Someone is always there for you, someone is always going to listen—you just have to find that someone you trust.

Make sure you plan things to look forward to, such as outings with friends. Be a supportive and loving friend, and your friends will support and love you in return.

As a result of seeking help, I understand myself better now, and I'm able to recognise if my mind starts to slip into negativity. If that happens, I ask myself, 'What can I do to turn it around?'

Remind yourself that when you wake up tomorrow, it's a new day.

True beauty is on the inside—how you feel about yourself is so important. Learn to love who you are and what you stand for.

Abby

Life is about choice; it's all in your hands. People can advise you of options, but it's up to you to act upon it. Always stay true to yourself, because if you don't that's another day in your life you've spent doing what other people wanted you to do, not what you wanted.

I made mistakes and I learned from my lessons. I realised that when you don't get what you want, you get an experience. In order to better yourself and your life, you need to appreciate what you already have. And be patient because everything comes to those who wait, and I waited and slowly I'm getting stronger.

For such a long time in my life, I lived in darkness, where I felt like I was worthless and bad things were made especially for me. But because I survived so many emotional battles, I have complete faith that everyone in this world can get through anything. The only person you need is 'you'—a while ago when people would say that to me, I would laugh, but now I wish I'd understood the meaning of it when I was younger.

Veronica

If I could say one thing to myself when I was thirteen, I would say, 'You are stronger than you think you are, just trust yourself and never ever give up.' I'm still grieving, I still cry. But I look back at my life and know I can get through anything. All you need is you. You never really know how strong you are until being strong is the only choice you have. Your life is waiting for you and you choose when it begins.

Veronica

Speak up and know that people do care about you, and it's better to reach out and let them help you. It's so much better to talk than to bottle up your feelings. It only gets worse when you bottle things up; the problem is not going to go away by itself so make sure you talk to people you trust.

Emma

Evaluate your friends: If you need to talk to someone, don't risk telling the wrong person who might tell other people, as that will hurt even more. Tell the person who will keep your confidence—someone who has displayed a pattern of trust in the past. And the most important thing to remember is that life is too short to waste over the past. I have moved on and become a better woman for it. I am now living in a new apartment with my boyfriend, I have a fun exciting stable job and I have people around me to make me happy, not bring me down. You have so much to look forward to so set yourself up now for a happy successful life.

Alexis

Tip

When people love you for who you are, that's how you know they are your real friends—when they don't judge you.

Surround yourself with people who love you, people who are positive and happy.

You've got to want to change. No matter how many people want to help you to become a better person, unless you are prepared to make a change it won't happen.

Find the outlet that helps you, whether it is one-on-one counselling or a youth camp. I loved the youth camps because the leaders were teenagers who had come through trauma and been through the camps themselves. A lot of my answers came from teenagers on camp.

You can't expect life to turn around if you aren't prepared to try. And you've got to try. That's all you can do. Keep trying and never give up.

Bronte

Hang in there because everything's going to be okay.

I realised that you can't be helped unless you actually want to be helped and that if you look around, there could be other people going through similar things as you. Don't be afraid to open up to these people because if they have been there, they will be able to help you. Always ask for help if you need it.

Meg

The thing that helped me most was the support at the youth camp, and the love of my family. I know they will support me even when I make mistakes, and that making mistakes is all part of learning life lessons.

Speak up until someone listens. If you are feeling lost and alone, know there are people out there who will listen to you. Pick up the phone and call a helpline, or write your thoughts and feelings into a letter and post it to someone you trust who can help you.

Robert

I created an imaginary friend and this really helped me when I needed someone to vent to. Although he was in my imagination, I still played out the conversation and the way I was feeling, which gave me greater perspective.

Robert

If you are feeling down, frustrated or angry, talk to the people you trust. Try not to let anger get the better of you as that will just make the situation worse. Sometimes it helps to write down how you are feeling and then read it out aloud. This provides clarity.

Always aim to achieve what *you* want to achieve, and don't let anyone tell you that you can't do something.

Jessica

Know that it's okay to cry. Let it out, let yourself feel. Talk to people you trust and allow yourself to feel loved by others. You deserve to be loved.

Set goals that are important to you and try hard to stay focused on them.

Daniel

Keep talking to people until someone listens and takes you seriously. Always speak up if something is troubling you.

James

Don't let anyone force their opinion on you or push you into anything you don't want to do. Go with what feels right for you; listen to yourself and trust yourself. Set a boundary and stick to it.

Katie

Just keep going with your life. Listen to people who have been through what you are going through. Turn your situation into a positive by setting goals for yourself, so you always have something to work towards.

Don't stop trying and don't be afraid to take risks. If you reach out, you will find there will always be something out there. This I know for sure.

Murray

Never give up—your day will come to shine and, as I have learned, your soul and willpower are the strongest things in your body. They will help you to grow and blossom into a beautiful rose.

Alyssa-Kate

If a situation is getting you down, look outside what you are going through. Focus on the things in life that make you happy and talk about it with your real friends, the ones who stand by you and support you.

Friends should lift each other up—if someone does a good job, tell them, show them they are not worthless. Encourage people to do their best.

Remember, self-esteem starts with steadfast belief in yourself.

Simon

No family is perfect. My mum doesn't listen to me and I just have to find a way to deal with that. Every family has their flaws so find a way to deal with it that feels right for you.

Jess

I look back and think I was such an idiot to act that way. I didn't think of the repercussions. But there are always consequences to your actions. I thought I knew what I was doing—I thought I was so cool and had it all together—but I wasn't.

Remember who you are. Don't do things just because other people want you to and don't try to be someone you're not. Being a people pleaser will only make you unhappy.

When I was in that wild state, I was so blind to seeing what might happen in future. You need to live not just for now, but for the future as well. Be true to yourself and think about the future that feels right for you—the one you truly want.

If you worry about what others think, as long as people have that hold on you, you're not doing what you want to do or being who *you* want to be.

Natashia

Chapter 23

MOVING FORWARD

'Courage does not always roar. Sometimes it's a quiet voice at the end of the day saying "I will try again tomorrow".'

Mary Anne Radmacher

Life is indeed a rollercoaster. It's important to remember that living in a constant state of happiness is not a realistic expectation. While we can all learn to express ourselves, listen to our inner voice, and find our peace and happiness, there will always be bumps in the road, some more significant than others. It's a matter of embracing the landscape and allowing yourself to change and grow, to adjust with each kink in the road and accept where you are. Once you accept your circumstances, you can then take action to change them.

Melinda

I tend to over-think things. I suffered emotional abandonment and, as a result, learned to do everything on my own. I became very independent on a practical level, as well as emotionally independent. When I first got together with my boyfriend, he was so caring and attentive and interested in everything about me, it felt wonderful. But because of my newfound vulnerability, I fell into being dependent on him.

Thankfully, I realise when I'm in dependency mode now and have learned how to steer myself out of it. I look at my day-to-day routine to see where I'm compromising it to please or be around my boyfriend. If I recognise that I'm being dependent or smothering him, I change my routine so I do things on my own, as an individual, until I find my centre again.

Alexis

Tip
Let the voice that speaks from your heart empower you to make the decisions that feel right for the future you wish to create.

When I was young I liked to play with Barbie dolls and be their doctor. I'd break their arms and legs, and then fix them. So when I figured that sitting around doing nothing wasn't going to serve me on any level, the first thing I did was to get on my computer and research medical procedures. Then I started scrapbooking, which gave me something to do with my hands. This also got me moving about because I had to go downstairs to find scissors and glue, among other things. Once I started moving I found I couldn't sit down any longer. Having a project was a great distraction.

Alexis

Find a project. Start with something small, like organising your room, or drawing pictures. Getting lost in a project will take your mind off your problems which in turn will give you perspective.

Alexis

An idea is often promoted which says that we must know exactly where we are going before we take the first step. The net result is that some people spend their whole life waiting before they take the first step; some people take the step and when things don't work out the way they had intended, they spend their days disappointed and despondent.

I go with the idea that the important thing is just to start. Find something that you love to do and just start doing it. If you don't know what it is yet, think about it or spend some time exploring that. (A good step might be to ask people around you three things they think you're good at. It's surprising how much people can see in us that sometimes we can't see in ourselves.)

When you find something that you love to do, do it over and over, learn about it. See how it relates to other things. Lose yourself in it and find a way to do it that makes a contribution to something and to someone.

Tom

I go through phases—sometimes I'm angry at my dad, other times I want to tell him how well I'm going. At the end of the day he is manipulative, and the emotional price I would have to pay to have any kind of relationship with him is too high. I have to keep reminding myself what he's really like and how relieved I felt the day I stopped speaking to him. I could ring and ask him for $100 tomorrow and he'd give it to me. Not having money has been hard, but the sacrifice has been worth it, because in return I have saved myself and I love my life.

Amy

> ## Tip
> There is no point thinking too far ahead or worrying about the future. If you take care of the present moment, the future will take care of itself. All we have is 'now'. If you come from a place of 'anything is possible', this will lessen the fear of the unknown and replace it with a sense of excitement about the endless possibilities for your future.

I have come to realise that Mum works hard so she can financially support me and my sister, not because she wants to abandon us, and I have a renewed respect for her.

I tell Mum I love her, and she tells me she loves me. We have a different relationship now. I can look back and see that

I have come a long way from the scared, lonely little girl who cried herself to sleep at night.

Mum told me I've changed, that I've turned myself around, and she believes me now when I tell her if something is hurting me. She knows I was in incredible pain and the fact that she has acknowledged this has helped me move forward. Knowing that I have her support means so much to me. She is always telling me I can talk to her if I need to, and encouraging me to do my best. I know that she loves and accepts me for who I am and this means the world to me.

Emma

Mum has leukaemia now, and another fiancé. She's moved away. We still have a relationship but she's hurt me so many times that I am tired of it. I go through stages where I'm happier if we're not communicating.

I've learned to be happy with who I am. I see things more openly. I've been through things not many adults have had to deal with their whole lifetime and it's made me strong and focused. I know I can handle anything life throws at me.

I feel so strong now. It took so much work. My old group of friends gave me a second chance because they could see how hard I was trying. They believed in me again and that made me feel good.

Natashia

Through attending youth camps and talking things out with my support person from these camps, I've learned how to change the way I choose to behave. I learned to ignore Mum's behaviour when it was wrong and acknowledge it when it was right. I learned how to stand up for myself so that Mum would listen.

One time she went to hit me and I grabbed her hand and said, 'You do not hit your children'. And she stared at me, gobsmacked, like I was a stranger. I said, 'If you're angry you need to tell me why so we can work through it.'

That made me feel as though I'd done something positive for myself.

The youth camps taught me strategies to mentor my mum. Since I've adopted these strategies, Mum tries harder. If she doesn't know how to do something, she comes to me and knocks on my door, which in itself is astounding, considering I spent two weeks without a door knob at one stage to stop her barging in and yelling at me whenever she felt like it.

When I had anger building, Mum would feed off that anger. She wouldn't accept what I was trying to tell her. I have learned how to control my anger, and how to better communicate with Mum. She knows when she can't be around us now, and will stay in her room, but still listen to everything going on in the house. In her own way she's trying and I respect her for this.

Mum learning to communicate in a productive way has brought our family closer. We are protective of her and now know when it's a good day for Mum and when she is having a stressful or unhappy day, and we have learned how to work around this. We love our mum and we know we need her good days in our family. And until every day is a good day, we will look after her. It's not a chore anymore; we all want to do it, we all love her so much and we see Dad's love for her too.

Bronte

After my first youth camp I quit drugs, after my second I quit smoking and after the third I decided to stop drinking. I am now back home with my mum and things are going well.

When I started school this year, the teacher I had last year came up to me and told me that my attitude towards school had changed completely and that I'm so positive now. That made me happy and encouraged me to work harder.

I was selected to undergo leadership training for Youth Insearch. It was absolutely amazing. I met some really great people and gained self-confidence.

I have been chosen do to a peer skills program with the school through Lifeline. It really surprised me that people voted me as a person they could approach for advice if they had a problem. I felt very proud of myself and excited, and a bit nervous.

Meg

I have to go to court in a few months and talk about what happened when my friend's dad tried to rape me. At first I felt scared and didn't want to do it but now I believe that it's going to make me stronger. I want to do it so I can honour myself.
Meg

I've discovered a way of life that is fulfilling: live to be a better person, to help other people and to inspire others.

I'm so happy in my life now. I'm popular at this new school and I haven't been bullied once. The environment is very much one of mutual respect and encouragement. Everyone is supportive, especially when it comes to performance. I'm not very confident with singing, and so many people have offered to help me with this. I'm finally living my dream. I cannot imagine where I'll be in twelve months' time let alone a few weeks.

Robert

I've been with my grandma since I was six, so for nine years now. I have recently developed a new bond with my mother. She ended up divorcing her husband after he started physically assaulting her. Fortunately, she's now with a decent partner and we are attempting to re-establish a relationship.

At times I do feel as though my life is being dictated to me. My mother doesn't support my hopes and dreams. Everytime I tell her I want to do something, she tells me why I won't succeed. This upsets me because I feel she doesn't really know who I am.

My whole life, all I ever wanted was to feel needed and wanted. Because I felt unloved and abandoned, I went through a period of extreme anger, which turned into chronic anger. But through counselling, I learned that masking my emotions isn't healthy, and the only way to get through something is to face it head on and try to deal with it in a positive way. Slowly, I'm learning to come to terms with my situation.

Jessica

I'm focusing on my goals and the life that I want to build for myself. I want to become a youth leader to help other teenagers who are going through trauma, and when I finish school I want to join the army. Then I want to study greenkeeping so I can spend my time among nature. I love gardening. It is the perfect peaceful place I can go and 'be'.

Daniel

I know how my parents feel about me—they think I'm a murderer. They didn't want the family to have a bad name, or people gossiping about the fact that their daughter was pregnant at fifteen. But I also know that a lot of their insecurities stem from their own issues. So mostly it is about them, not me. I'm now a youth counsellor for the local shire council, representing young people in the area. I'm living with my nan and call her place 'home'.

Katie

I'm thirteen years old now and living with my nan. She knows me so well, and it feels great to be in a place where I know I'm safe, and I'm not going to be tempted to get into any trouble out of frustration from watching my mum abuse drugs and alcohol. Or from the pain of having two fathers suicide and feeling as though I'm unloved and not important.

I've learned that if I'm going to have a good future, it's up to me, and no-one else. Only I can change my situation.

Murray

As a result of being sexually abused by my dad, I became a non-religious celibate. This means I'm keeping my virginity

282

until marriage and not for religious purposes. My belief was that if my father could take advantage of me, then anybody could—originally I hid behind the invisible wall of celibacy any time a male came close to me. Now I have knocked that defensive wall down and no longer hide behind anything—I'm just proud that I respect myself to remain a virgin and that means the world to me. Last Christmas my parents bought me a bracelet and a ring. I asked for their permission to convert that ring from a Christmas present from my family into something just as meaningful and treasured to me—a purity ring, which enforces my belief in abstinence.

Despite everything I still love both my parents and have forgiven them for all that's happened over the years.

I choose to look at my life with gratitude, because without all the mountains to climb at such a young age, I wouldn't be the person I am today, or know who I want to be.

I want to go to university and become an English and social studies teacher for secondary students, as well as a youth counsellor, so I can help the future youth.

My past has given me the gift to heal myself and others around me. I'm able to change a negative into a positive and move on from it—the construction of a bridge that I can eventually cross and leave the other side behind.

Alyssa-Kate

Forgiveness can be a difficult and challenging thing to do especially when you're forgiving someone's actions that have hurt you deeply or have led you to no longer trust them again. However, it lays your soul on a bed of peace and harmony and, in leaving your past behind you, allows you to get one step closer to creating a better future for yourself.

Alyssa-Kate

Chapter 24

STEERING THE PATH TO YOUR FUTURE

'Do not go where the path may lead. Go instead
where there is no path and leave a trail.'
Ralph Waldo Emerson

It *is* possible to make your dreams come true! Spend some
time thinking about the kind of future you'd like to create for
yourself. What action can you take to start paving the way to
the future of your dreams? If you don't know what you want
to do just yet, that's okay too. As long as you're doing the
things that bring you joy and make you happy, your life will
be enriched and you'll naturally feel a sense of contentment.

Melinda

I've studied make-up artistry and beauty therapy, and I'm still
unsure what direction I want to pursue. But I'm not scared

about not knowing what I want to do with my future. I was drilled my whole life that 'You've got to do your HSC and go to university to be someone.' I hated school so left after Year 10 and now I love life because I'm living it on my terms, not to please other people.

Alexis

I'm studying social science and majoring in criminology and psychology. Psychology is related to everything I've been through and I want to help other people deal with hardship and help them find a way out.

Lauren

I've worked hard to become successful. I have my own business and I'm doing a Masters degree. To me, the idea of success is simply discovering what you love to do, discovering what you're good at doing (or what you can become good at doing), and finding a way to do that which contributes to a cause.

Tom

I now train Lifeline counsellors and present at conferences to increase the awareness of self-injury among teenagers. I know my scars from self-injury are always going to be there. There's no point running away from them. I've come to accept them as a part of who I am.

Amy

I'm applying to TAFE to study beauty therapy or make-up. It helps to have a goal to look forward to, especially one that I'm so passionate about.

Abby

Life seems more normal these days. Every now and then a hiccup arises but generally speaking, in the grand scheme of things, it's nothing compared to what I once thought was 'normal'. I've always questioned what 'normal' is.

Currently I'm training for leadership with Youth Insearch, which was created for peers to help peers and to help put lives of teens who've had difficult life experiences or upbringings back on track and shower them in the basic necessities that all children deserve, such as love and support.

Unfortunately, the reality is not all kids get this during their childhood and I want to help those kids who suffered neglect and abuse as I did and don't believe they're worthy of love. Like me they deserve a new chance at life—another chance to create their own story from scratch.

Alyssa-Kate

Tip

Create affirmation cards. Get your friends together and have each person write their name on the top of an index card. Then pass the index cards around so everyone writes down one thing they love about each person on their card. Read each one aloud. Keep your affirmation card with you and refer to it often.

Chapter 25

YOU ARE ENOUGH

'Nothing splendid has ever been achieved except
by those who dared believe that something
inside of them was superior to circumstance.'

Bruce Barton

It's not what happens to us, it's what we do with it that counts.
How we choose to live, to treat ourselves, and others, is a
reflection of who we are and what we stand for.

Don't let anyone tell you that you aren't good enough and
if they do, refuse to take it on.

Always tell yourself: I am enough.

'Inspiration unleashes a magical energy; the
promise that anything is possible.'

Melinda

Believe in who you are because you are magnificent. Let the thoughts that speak from your heart empower you. You are loved. You deserve happiness.

The future is yours; reach for the stars and let your light shine.

Melinda

NOTES

1. Australian Bureau of Statistics (ABS), 2007
2. Australian Bureau of Statistics (ABS), 2004
3. Burke, S., McIntosh, J., & Gridley, H. (2007), *Parenting after separation: A position statement prepared for the Australian Psychological Society*. Melbourne: Australian Psychological Society.
4. Australian Bureau of Statistics (ABS). 'Causes of Death' [Cat. no. 3303.0], 2008. Canberra, Commonwealth of Australia.
5. Habbo body image survey, 3 September 2009. www.habbo.com.au
6. Australian Institute of Health and Welfare (AIHW), 2007, 'Young Australians: Their health and wellbeing', Australian Institute of Health and Welfare (AIHW), Canberra, Cat. no. PHE 87.
7. Children, Youth and Women's Health (2009), *Self-harm*. Retrieved 11 March 2009, http://www.cyh.com/HealthTopics/HealthTopicDetails.aspx?p=243&np=293&id=2464

8. RANZCP (2005), *Self-harm. Australian Treatment Guide for Consumers and Carers.* Melbourne: The Royal Australian and New Zealand College of Psychiatrists.

9. Hawton, K., Zahl, D., & Weatherall, R. (2003), 'Suicide following deliberate self-harm: long term follow-up of patients who presented to a general hospital', *British Journal of Psychiatry, 182,* 537—542.

10. Children, Youth and Women's Health (2009), *op cit.*

11. Stanley, B., Gameroff, M., Michalsen, V. & Mann, J. (2001), 'Are suicide attempters who self-mutilate a unique population?', *American Journal of Psychiatry, 158 (3),* 427–432.

12. Farrand, J. & Solomon, Y. (1996), 'Why don't you do it properly? Young women who self-injure', *Journal of Adolescence,* 19 (2), 111–119

13. Cox, T. (1995), 'Stress coping and physical health', in A. Broome and S. Llewelyn (eds), *Health Psychology: Process and Application.* London: Singular Publication Group; Rigby, K. (1998), *The relationship between reported health and involvement in bully/victim problems among male and female secondary school students.* Journal of Health Psychology, 3(4), 465–476; Rigby, K. (1999). Bullying—no way! . . . a commentary. Educational Views, 26 March.

14. Kids Helpline (2004)

15. Research carried out at Australian Catholic University's (ACU National) Canberra Campus. The study involved nearly 700 students in years 7 to 10 and more than 160 teachers and took place over thirteen months.

16. (Microsoft/Galaxy Research, 2008) http://today.ninemsn. com.au/article.aspx?id=840251

ACKNOWLEDGEMENTS

Within the pages of this book the heart and soul of many inspiring individuals have been bared in the hope of helping others. It has been a huge project that would not have been possible without the support of so many amazing people.

I would especially like to thank:

My wonderful agent, Selwa Anthony, for her guidance, wisdom and friendship. Thank you so much for believing in me.

Maggie Hamilton, Publisher, Allen & Unwin, for her wonderful insights, unwavering support and inspiration, and whose friendship I count among my blessings.

The team at Allen & Unwin, especially Jo Lyons for her superb editorial advice, and Susin Chow, Christa Moffitt, Megan Johnston, Kathy Mossop, Andy Palmer and Emma Ward for their guidance, passion and commitment.

I am proud to be associated with many incredible people and organisations who are passionate about and dedicated to helping young people overcome hardship, including Ron and Judith Barr of Youth Insearch, particularly Judith for showing me such warmth and trust; Dan Geaves, Kerry Graham, Charlotte Beaumont-Field, Michelle Blanchard and Janice Atkin of the Inspire Foundation: Christine Morgan, Mary Orenstein and Julie Parker of the Butterfly Foundation; Wendy Protheroe and Marie Bryan of Kids Helpline; Captain Paul Moulds and Sandy Ludman of Oasis Youth Support Network; Karalee Evans and Vikki Ryall of headspace; and Jessica Brown and Lyndal Blom of Life Changing Experiences Foundation and the SISTER2sister program. I am also grateful to Ramesh Manocha, Dianne McKissock, Tessa Marshall, Margaret Condonis, Carolyn Rae, Chris Basten, Dianne Fitzjames and Jeremy Freeman for their involvement and support.

To all the people I interviewed, your courage is boundless and your strength indomitable, and your willingness to share past hurts in order to bring love and healing to others is truly inspiring.

Kris Teece, for putting me in touch with so many people, and for your friendship. You are a success story all of your own.

Louise Killeen, you are truly magnificent. Your strength, heart and spirit is an inspiration to me.

Cath Healy, for being incredibly wise and wonderful.

Alana Ruben Free, for inspiring women everywhere to live their truth, and for your love and friendship.

To all my beautiful friends, your love, wisdom, encouragement and support mean so much to me. I'd like to make special mention of Tara Moss, Jacinta Tynan, Belinda Alexandra, Wendy Nichols, Lyn McPherson, Libby-Jane Charleston and Lucinda Guy.

To my parents, Carol and Vic, for a lifetime of love and wisdom; to Felicity, Julia and Geoff, for always being there; and Trudie, Renee, Chris, Emma, Maddie and cousin-to-be. I love you all dearly.

And to my precious Flynn, who brings me endless joy and happiness; every moment I spend with you is a gift.

I am truly blessed to have such wonderful people in my life who mean the world to me and without whom none of this would be possible.

Melinda Hutchings